leader's

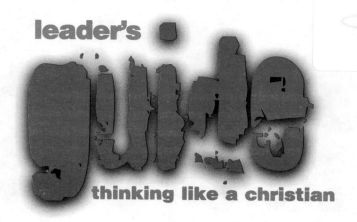

thinking like a christian

david noebel
chuck edwards

summit press
manitou springs, colorado 80829

Copyright ©1999 by Summit Ministries
Summit Press, P.O. Box 207, Manitou Springs, Colorado 80829
(719) 685-9103
www.summit.org

Unless indicated otherwise, Scripture quotations are from the Holy Bible, *New International Version,* ©1973, 1978, 1984 by the International Bible Society.

ISBN 0-936163-07-0

preface

by best selling author and speaker
josh mcdowell

You are holding in your hands one of the most important youth Bible studies to come out in recent years. I don't say that lightly. Let me explain why I believe that is so.

At this very moment, we are right in the center of one of the greatest, deepest, and most rapid cultural changes ever in history. It started when the radical students of the sixties began taking over the universities. By the 80's, things had progressed to the point that Francis Schaeffer stated that we no longer live in a Judeo-Christian culture, but a post-Christian culture.

Cultural change is all around us. Nowhere is it more evident than on our university campuses. In the last 35 years, I've given over 23,000 talks in over 1,000 universities in 100 countries around the world. And what I'm finding is this: these universities — which once had as their purpose the passing on of truth and wisdom to the next generation — now have as their mission the indoctrination of young people into an wholly different way of life. It comes out of a "humanist" view of life, that is, ideas about the meaning and purpose of life are based on man's perspective instead of on God's.

The challenge for you and for me is to prepare a generation of young people who can understand the times and who will know what to do. This means showing them that being a Christian is more then just having a personal experience with God — it means seeing all of life in light of God's truth. It means developing a consistent biblical worldview.

That's why this curriculum is so important. It is uniquely designed to guide today's high school or college student into an encounter with a biblical worldview. David Noebel has spent over 35 years teaching these concepts to thousands of young people who have come through **The Summit** conferences each summer. It is an eye-opening experience that has changed the lives of countless youth.

My own son was one of those who came face to face with a biblical worldview at **The Summit**. It was by far one of the most significant conferences he has ever attended. The impact will affect Sean the rest of his life. My seventeen year old daughter Katie went through a similar curriculum in her high school. This has prepared her for college-- not only to survive-- but also to thrive in her walk with Christ.

Now, through this new curriculum, thousands more youth will be challenged to understand the times in which we live. Then, like the men from the small tribe of Issachar in 1 Chronicles 12:32, they will know what they should do.

I wish you the best as you train the next generation of Christians to understand the times.

josh

mapping out the journey

worldviews in focus
thinking like a christian

IDEAS FOR THE BIBLE STUDY LEADER

This course lays the foundation of a "biblical worldview." You and those you teach will find this an exciting adventure as the full view of a biblical understanding of all of life comes into focus.

This study of worldview, seeking to cover ten major disciplines in a 12 week period, is an expansive one. But don't let the scope be intimidating. While each of the ten disciplines (theology, philosophy, biology, psychology, ethics, sociology, law, politics, economics and history) takes a lifetime of study to understand fully, the uniqueness of David Noebel's book, *Understanding the Times*, is its ability to summarize each discipline in a simple and understandable way.

This course draws out the foundational principle upon which each discipline is built. Students will easily grasp the significance of these diverse subjects and relate each one to basic biblical principles. This foundation is necessary before the edifice of personal Christian living and involvement with society can be erected. As with the men of the small tribe of Issachar found in 1 Chronicles 12:32, we must first "understand the times" before we will "know what to do."

easy directions will help you lay a solid foundation
1) **read** the short chapter in *Understanding the Times* that corresponds with the lesson being taught.
2) **gather** the suggested materials for handouts and object lessons.
3) **review** the lesson outline. It is written in "scripted" form to give you a flavor of how to lead the class. **Feel free to use your own words!**

overview of curriculum
A. **GROUP MEETINGS:** The Group Meetings are designed with two parts to fit into either a 90-minute or 45-minute format.

1. **PART ONE - REVIEW:** There is a "REVIEW" section at the beginning of each lesson, starting with Lesson 2. The REVIEW is designed to reinforce the concepts from the previous week's group meeting and the daily assignments in the **Student Journal.** This gives you the opportunity to answer any questions students have about that topic. In addition, the review helps those who missed the previous week to catch up with the rest of the group. This REVIEW should take about 20-30 minutes.

2. **PART TWO - NEW TOPIC:** The second part of the group meeting introduces the NEW TOPIC in the series. This 40-50 minute session lays the groundwork for understanding the new category (such as Theology, Philosophy, etc.) through several interactive methods. It is designed to focus on a primary aspect of that discipline and to motivate students for further study in their journals.

3. By including both parts, "Review" and "New Topic," the entire group meeting should take about 90 minutes. If this curriculum is used for Sunday School or other shorter Bible study where time is limited, then the "Review" section can be omitted, leaving the 45-minute "New Topic" as the focus of the lesson.

B. **STUDENT JOURNALS:** The Student Journal is designed as a resource to expand and enhance the student's understanding of the issues discussed during the group meetings. The five daily assignments give a broader perspective related to that week's worldview category. **Educational studies confirm that this type of "spaced repetition" insures the best retention of new information. In our secular culture, it is imperative that students take to heart these important biblical concepts.**

To motivate students to do their journal assignments, plan a pizza party or other special event at the end of the course. Tell students at the beginning of the study that anyone who completes the journal can attend the special event. It's best to have students bring in their journals each week to check their progress. In that way, this will remind them to be consistent and not fall behind.

overview of the twelve weeks
1. **introduction** What's a biblical worldview?
2. **theology** What about God?
3. **philosophy** What is reality?
4. **biology** What about life?
5. **psychology** What about human nature?
6. **ethics** What's right?
7. **sociology** What about relationships?
8. **law** What are the rules?
9. **politics** What about government?
10. **economics** What about money?
11. **history** What about the past?
12. **conclusion** Putting it all together: Thinking like a Christian!

suggestions for digging deeper
INITIAL PREPARATION

Because of the scope of this course, you should begin preparing in advance of the time to teach. This is especially true if this is the first time you have taught these concepts. The following two suggestions will give you a basic background for this course:

1. STUDY THE MAIN TEXTBOOK: Read the Introduction to *Understanding the Times* (Abridged Edition), Chapters 1 & 2. These two chapters point out the importance of this study and demonstrate the significance of understanding Christianity from a "worldview" perspective. It also points out that there are other worldviews vying for our attention, namely Secular Humanism, Cosmic Humanism (New Age) and Marxism. These three worldviews will be taught in a separate study course. The focus for this twelve-week session is the **Biblical Christian** worldview.

    Next, read each of the chapters on Biblical Christianity under each section (i.e. Theology, Philosophy, etc). This will give you a sense of the scope and direction of the course. It also will help you to implement the next idea: setting up a simple filing system.

2. KEEP IT CURRENT: Students want to know that what they are studying is relevant to their lives. The best way to accomplish this is to show them examples from current events. This opens their eyes to the significance of what is being taught and heightens their interest in the ideas being presented. It also takes learning out of the monochrome dustbin of history and splashes it into the technicolor world of "now," linking past with present!

thinking like a christian

A. **EXPAND YOUR RESOURCES:** In order to have current illustrations, look for articles in the daily paper or weekly magazines that relate to the ten categories of the course. Articles may either confirm the biblical view or illustrate an opposing view. It is recommended that you subscribe to a conservative or Christian source in order to gain a balanced perspective on the news. Check out the list at the end of this introduction for some suggestions.

B. **SET UP A FILING SYSTEM:** A simple filing system can be started to keep track of current articles.

☐ Purchase a plastic file box and set of 10 three-cut file folders.

☐ Label each file according to the ten categories of this course, "THEOLOGY," "PHILOSOPHY," etc.

☐ As you read an article, write in the top left-hand corner the category it relates to, tear it out, and place it in the appropriate file. Then, for example, when you teach the lesson on "Biology," you can look in that file for current examples of the creation/evolution debate.

weekly preparation

1. **PLAN AHEAD:** As you can see, this course does not lend itself to waiting until the last minute to prepare the lesson. You should set aside some time several days throughout the week to prepare for each week's lesson. Reading the text and reviewing the Leader's Guide are a part of that preparation.

2. **STAY CURRENT:** Continue to look in the newspapers, including the comic sections, for current illustrations to use in class. Throughout the course of study, you will be encouraging students to do the same. Each week, let them show you what they found before you bring out any articles. Discuss the articles with them informally before or after class.

3. **USE THE STUDENT JOURNAL:** The **Student Journal** parallels each week's lesson and contains excerpts from the corresponding chapter in *Understanding the Times*. However, it is arranged in a new way with illustrations that are not in the text. You will want to read and do the daily assignments along with the students. This will give you additional insights as you prepare for the review session.

The above suggestions will help you feel prepared and equipped. The students in your group will pick up on your enthusiasm for the content and respond with renewed interest of their own. "Boring" will drop from their vocabulary!

We wish you the best in your efforts to prepare the coming generation to understand the times in which we live and play an active role in being "salt and light" to our tasteless and dark society.

We're praying for you,

David Noebel & Chuck Edwards

resource list

You may want to try one or more of the following resources. While we do not endorse everything that is printed in these resources, they generally will give a conservative, biblically-oriented perspective on current events. (Prices are subject to change)

1. **The Journal:** A monthly publication from Summit Ministries, edited by David A. Noebel, the author of the textbook used for this course. It includes excerpts from books and articles dealing with all ten disciplines covered in this course, and representing all four worldviews: Biblical, Humanist, Marxist, and Cosmic Humanist (New Age). It costs Summit Ministries approximately $15 per year per subscription. Call (719) 685-9103.

2. **World Magazine:** A weekly news resource from a Christian publisher. It covers current local, state, national and worldwide issues in the news from a Christian perspective. $49.95/year. Call (800) 951-6397. www.worldmag.com.

3. **Breakpoint:** A monthly commentary on faith and culture presented by Chuck Colson. It is an excellent, concise treatment of ideas from every area of study. $45.00/year. (800) 457-6125.

4. **Human Events:** A weekly conservative newspaper with articles and commentaries on national and international news. It is a counter-balance to the liberal press' biased reporting on current issues. $50.00/year introductory rate. (800)787-7557.

5. **Citizen:** The monthly magazine from Focus on the Family dealing with a variety of current issues related to Christian morality, government and the family. $20.00/year. (800) 232-6459.

6. **The Real Issue:** A 10-page bulletin published five times a year by Christian Leadership Ministries, the faculty ministry of Campus Crusade for Christ. It deals with current trends on university campuses with subjects that range from the creation/evolution debate to the "politically correct" wars on campus. This is very important information for students who attend state-supported universities. No charge. (214) 490-7770.

7. **Imprimis:** A 6-page publication from Hillsdale College featuring a monthly article from a conservative author who is knowledgeable in a particular area. A wide range of issues are covered from month to month including economics, law, politics, education, etc. No charge. (800) 437-2268.

8. **Campus:** Published three times a year, this conservative publication is written and edited by college students. Each issue describes current happenings (everything from "Condom week" to liberal professors to homosexual demands, etc.) on college campuses across America. No charge to students and faculty. All others $10.00/year. (800) 526-7022.

BIBLIOGRAPHY: Main text: *Understanding the Times*, David A. Noebel. Other resources: *How Should We Now Live, Against the Night* and *Kingdoms in Conflict*, Chuck Colson; *Children At Risk*, James Dobson; *Lifeviews*, R. C. Sproul; *Making Sense of Your World*, W. Gary Phillips & William E. Brown; *The Universe Next Door*, James Sire; *A Christian Manifesto*, Francis Schaeffer.

thinking like a christian

overview
lesson 1

what's a biblical worldview?

The introductory group lesson is intended to orient students to the whole concept of a "worldview." Most have never thought in those terms. It is truly a mind-expanding experience!

This first session, as well as each group session, is designed to focus on a single issue by coming at it from various angles. This approach reinforces the objectives for lasting impact.

It usually takes three or four weeks before most students "catch" the vision. Lights will start clicking on as they realize that their faith is an all-encompassing view of reality. Don't be discouraged if they don't "get it" in the first week or two. You are leading them up a mountain in order to give them a panorama view of life's issues. You are introducing them to a whole new way of looking at life through the lens of Scripture. The sequence used in this course will guide them through the process. Encourage them to do their daily assignments, to come to the group meetings, and most will respond positively as they see the relevancy of each lesson.

You are about to embark on a great adventure! **Be of good courage and may God bless your efforts!**

lesson one

introduction to a biblical worldview

key concept: Jesus is the basis of a Christian worldview.

key verses: Colossians 2:6-8
"So then, just as you received Christ Jesus as Lord, continue to live in him, rooted and built up in him, strengthened in the faith as you were taught, and overflowing with thankfulness. See to it that no one takes you captive through hollow and deceptive philosophy, which depends on human tradition and the basic principles of this world rather than on Christ."

objectives: By the end of this lesson, each student should be able to
. . . explain how the Bible is as current as today's newspaper and relates to all areas of life.
. . . defend the concept that a follower of Christ considers all of life sacred.

background study:

Understanding the Times (Abridged Edition), (referred to in future lessons as "UTT") by David A. Noebel
Read Chapters 1-2.

before class:

☐ Copy handout A so that every student (OR PAIR) has a puzzle. Cut the puzzle into separate pieces and place each set in a separate envelope marked "Puzzle."

☐ Make enough copies of handout B for each student to have one SET of words/pictures. Cut out each word and symbol, scramble the order and place in an envelope marked "Worldview."

☐ For III. A. "Headline News," look through the newspaper during the week and find articles that deal with different topics. Have at least one article per student. It's easier to handle if you tape each article to a 8 1/2 X 11 piece of paper. Review III. A.5 for examples of how these articles will be used and what you need to say about each one.

☐ Have a pencil for each student and push-pins or scotch tape for the articles.

☐ Draw the outline of the completed puzzle on the board and cover it with a piece of paper large enough to hide it from view.

☐ Have a cassette tape or CD player to play the song by Audio Adrenaline, *My World View* (if available).

☐ Make a copy for each student of the handouts, **"My World View," "Genesis Study," "Categories that make a Worldview,"** and if teaching high school students, the **"Parent Up-Date"** Letter.

☐ Have a **STUDENT JOURNAL** to give each student in the group.

note:

What the teacher says is in **bold type.** *Remember, the scripted format is to aid you in your study.*
Use your own words during the actual lesson. Suggested answers to questions are in (. . .).

I. INTRODUCTION:

   A. PUZZLE ACTIVITY: Give to each student an envelope with the puzzle pieces inside.

      1. SAY: **See if you can put the pieces of this puzzle together to form a square, that is, all sides equal. Let's see who can do it the fastest. You'll have 2 minutes.**

      2. Stop after 2 minutes and SAY: **Would it help if you had this?** Show completed puzzle outlined on the board or overhead. (Yes.) **Why?** (Because we know what the completed puzzle looks like.)

      3. SAY: **This picture of the completed puzzle I'll call the "Big Picture." Write the words, "BIG PICTURE," above the puzzle. Once you see the "big picture," it's easy to see how the smaller parts fit together.**

   B. SAY: **Life is like this puzzle. It's easier to understand the different parts if you can see the "big picture." ASK: If this whole puzzle were your life, what would the individual pieces represent?** (List on the board as they respond: relationships, school, faith in God, family, church, etc. Write these on both sides of the puzzle and draw lines to the various pieces.)

   C. SAY: **Our problem is that we tend to think only of the individual pieces, the small individual parts of life, fragmented pieces scattered about. We don't think about how they all fit into the larger picture of life. The fact is, all of these ideas are interconnected, interrelated to form a larger view of life.**

   D. TRANSITION: **What is the "big picture" that makes sense of and gives meaning to the individual parts? In order to understand this, we need to define a new word. That word is "WORLDVIEW."** Write the word "WORLDVIEW" across the puzzle. **But exactly what is a "worldview"?**

II. WORLDVIEW DEFINITION:

   A. SENTENCE SCRAMBLE: Pass out the envelopes containing Handout B, "Worldview."

      1. SAY: **Open your envelope and see if you can unscramble the words and symbols to form a sentence that would define the term "worldview." You'll have 3 minutes to work on this.** Walk around and help them think through arranging the words and symbols into one of the following sentences:

"A (total) (way) of (looking) at the (world)"

OR

"A (way) of (looking) at the (total) (world)"

      2. NOTE: Don't let this drag on for more than 2-3 minutes. Reveal the definition to the entire class. If someone arrives at the right answer, congratulate him/her and share their definition with the rest of the group.

   B. SAY: **A worldview is your belief system - a total way of looking at the world, the way you understand reality, or what the world is all about. A worldview is the "Big Picture" of life, and it is a coherent view that gives meaning to the individual pieces of your life.**

C. ASK: **Where do the ideas come from that make up your worldview?** (Parents/teachers.) **Where do their ideas come from?** (If they respond, "The Bible," stimulate their thinking by saying that the Bible is just about your relationship with God, right? See if they can defend the idea that the Bible relates to ALL of life. If they don't respond "The Bible," prompt them to say it.)

D. **"MY WORLD VIEW" SONG:** Hand each student a copy of "My World View" as you SAY: **Actually you're right. As Christians, we get our understanding of the world from the Bible. Listen to this song by Audio Adrenaline called, "My World View." As I play the song, follow the words.** NOTE: If you don't have access to the music, just use the handouts.

   1. ASK: **How do they define "worldview"?** (It's how I see the world; it's how I look at you.) Discuss these two aspects of a worldview with the group by asking questions such as:

      a. **What areas of your life would be included in the phrase, "how I see the world"?** (Various answers.)

      b. **What would be included in the second phrase, "how I look at you"?** (Various answers.)

   2. ASK: **What is the basis for the Worldview revealed in the words of this song?** (Jesus.)

      a. **Colossians 2:6-8:** Have students turn in their Bibles to Colossians 2:6-8. Call on someone to read the verses and discuss the following:
      (1) **What is meant by human philosophy?**
      (2) **In what ways are we captured by human philosophy?**
      (3) **How is Jesus the basis for building a worldview or biblical philosophy of life?**

      b. SUMMARY: Summarize what has been said so far concerning what a worldview is and how Jesus relates to developing a worldview. However, do not give away the answer to the question you are about to ask next.

E. TRANSITION: **But does the Bible relate to ALL of the different issues of life? To answer that question, let's look at this week's newspaper.**

III. THE BIBLE HAS A WORLDVIEW:

A. HEADLINE NEWS: Draw a line down the middle of a bulletin board (or down the middle of the floor). On the left side, write the heading "Relates to the Bible." On the right side, write the heading "Does not relate to the Bible." Let each student chose one article that you have previously cut out of the past week's newspapers.

   1. SAY: **Read the article and determine what the article is about in a general way.**

      a. **For example, if the article is a wedding announcement, it doesn't matter who. What we are looking for is the general subject of the article: "marriage."**

thinking like a christian

b. **Then, decide whether the Bible has anything to say about that idea or subject. If it does, tape (or place) your article on the left side of the bulletin board (or floor) under the heading: "Relates to the Bible." If you think that your article does not relate to the Bible, then tape/place it to the right side of the board/floor under the heading: "Does NOT relate to the Bible."** Allow time for everyone to place their article on the board.

2. DISCUSS: Start with one of the articles under the heading "Relates to the Bible."
ASK: **Which of you had this article? What is your article about, what's the big idea of it?** After he responds, ASK: **Does the Bible have anything to say about that topic?** Continue to point out articles and ask the same questions, prompting where needed, until all the articles on that side have been discussed.

3. "DOES NOT RELATE" SIDE: Discuss each of the articles under the heading "Does NOT Relate to the Bible." ASK: **Who had this article? What is your article about, what's the subject?** After he responds, ask: **Does the Bible have anything to say about that topic?** (various answers) Lead the discussion by telling how the general subject of each article relates to one of the categories on the handout "Categories that make a Worldview." Don't show them the handout yet. Use it as your guide in summarizing the subject of each article.

4. ARRANGE ARTICLES: As each article is discussed, move it over to the "Relates to the Bible" side. Rearrange articles as discussion continues until all the articles are on the "Relates to the Bible" side. SAY: **By placing all the articles on the "Relates to the Bible" side, we have drawn a very important conclusion here. We have discovered that everything in life relates to ideas found in the Bible. They all have religious, or sacred, implications. We see that there are no secular events; all are sacred because they are part of our total Christian worldview.**

5. NOTE: Try to find articles that relate to each of the ten categories. It will help for you to think through all the articles before class to make sure you can relate them to at least one of the categories. REMINDER: Do not show the ten categories to your class yet. That will come later in the lesson. The following examples may help:

a. As this lesson was being written, an F.B.I. agent was arrested for being a double agent. Since the man was caught for lying, this article relates to "Ethics," an area that the Bible addresses.

b. Another article in the news concerned the crash of an airliner. The question this raises is "What was the cause of the accident?" While people are looking for a direct cause, it also matters if you believe in God or not. Is God in sovereign control of everything that happens? This article relates to "Theology." The Bible addresses this issue.

c. Don't let the above discussion go too long. Keep the discussion brief and to the point. The issue here is not to elaborate on each article, but only to make the point that the Bible relates to the subject matter of each article. Practice this with your spouse or friends at work! It's a great mental exercise.

6. SUMMARY: **As you can see, the Bible is as current as today's newspaper! The Bible relates to ALL areas of your life.**

B. CATEGORIES THAT MAKE A WORLDVIEW:

1. HANDOUT: Give each student the handout titled "Categories That Make A"Worldview." SAY: **Each of these categories is a major discipline of study. They each focus on primarily one or two themes. These themes are expressed in our study by a short definition, and then a key question for that category.** Review with the class each of the ten categories. Have one student read aloud the definition and another read aloud the key question for each category.

2. SAY: **Each of these categories is like one piece of a puzzle. If we put these ten areas together, we would have a total view of the world. The Bible has something to say about each of these ten areas. To demonstrate that, we'll look at several chapters of the first book of the Bible, Genesis.**

C. GENESIS STUDY:

1. HANDOUT: Provide students pencils as you give them a handout on the "GENESIS STUDY." SAY: **Read the following verses to yourself and write in the categories that relate to each verse.** Allow 4 or 5 minutes

2. DISCUSS: After 5 minutes, ask what they put in the blanks. There may be more than one category that fits. Then SAY: **The Bible presents us with a personal relationship with God, and through the application of that relationship, shows us how we are to live in every area of our life. From this we see that every area of life relates back to God. Every area is religious, or sacred. Nothing in life is secular. The Bible gives us a total world and life view.**

D. 1 CHRONICLES 12:32: Call on someone to read it aloud.

1. SAY: **We are told that this small tribe in Israel was characterized by two things. What are they?** After they respond, summarize by SAYING: **First, they understood the times. Second, they knew what their nation should do.**

2. SAY: **Our goal for the next 12 weeks is to show you how the Bible relates to a total way of looking at the world so that you will be able to understand the times in which we live. Then you will be able to know what you should do with your life. You will learn how God can use you to impact the world!**

E. APPLICATION FOR THIS WEEK:

1. JOURNAL ASSIGNMENTS: Review the importance of doing the daily assignments in their STUDENT JOURNAL. Explain that the five daily assignments supplement and reinforce what they are learning in the group sessions.

   NOTE: You may want to check their progress each week and have a pizza party at the end of the course for all who have completed all or a percentage of all the lessons. Another idea would be to have a special "Graduation" ceremony for those who have completed the course. Be sure to tell them up front so they know what to expect. Make it fit your group. Be creative!

2. CLOSE IN PRAYER: Have everyone stand in a circle. Ask two or three to pray for everyone to understand the times in which we are living and for God to show them what they should do.

3. NOTE: If you are teaching high school students, include the following:

    a. LETTER TO PARENTS: Tell youth to take home a copy of the "Parent Up-Date" letter and give it to their parents. This will inform parents of the content of this unit of study.

    b. FAMILY PROJECT: Suggest that youth show their parents the handouts from today's lesson and share with them what was learned about how the Bible relates to life. Suggest a "Family Project": take Sunday's newspaper and have each member of the family look for an article and see if they can relate it to one of the ten categories that make up a worldview. **Bring one article next week to share with the rest of the class.**

---

important bulletin board idea for next session:

Before the next group meeting, draw a large puzzle with 10 pieces on a bulletin board or piece of paper, 4' x 6'. Label each piece with one of the worldview categories, i.e. Theology, Philosophy, etc. See enclosed "Sample Bulletin Board." You will use this each week to place the articles brought in by you or students. Each week, encourage students to find additional articles or ideas that relate to the area being studied, and tape them onto that piece of the puzzle. **This will serve as an object lesson for the entire 12 weeks.**

NOTE: Keep the newspaper articles you used this week. Have the articles available for the next group meeting for students to tape in the appropriate sections of the "worldview" puzzle bulletin board.

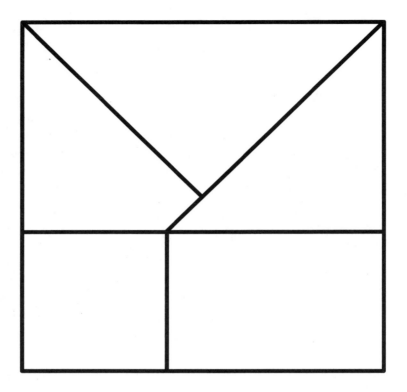

A   of

at the

A   of

at the

genesis study

Read each of the following passages from Genesis and write in the "worldview" category that relates to it. NOTE TO LEADER: While the verses do not develop the categories that are suggested, they do refer to the categories indicated. These categories are developed later in the Bible and by Christian thinkers who used principles of the Bible to elaborate and broaden the basic ideas. These biblical principles form the basis for the *Understanding The Times* study.

1:1 -   "In the beginning God..."   **theology**

1:1 -   "...God created the heavens and the earth..."   **theology/philosophy**

1:21 - "So God created the great creatures of the sea and every living
        and moving thing... according to its kind."   **biology**

2:7 -   "...and man became a living soul."   **psychology**

2:9 -   "...the tree of the knowledge of good and evil."   **ethics**

2:16 - "...the Lord God commanded the man,'...you must not eat from the tree...' "
                                                                          law/ethics

2:24 - "For this reason a man will leave his father and mother and be
        united to his wife..."   **sociology**

6:9 -   "This is the account of Noah..."   **history**

9:6 -   "Whoever sheds the blood of man, by man shall his blood be shed..." **politics**

42:3 - "Then ten of Joseph's brothers went down to buy grain from Egypt." **economics**

my world view

BY: Audio Adrenaline

I want to see the world through Jesus eyes, see through Jesus tears.
I want to see the world through Jesus eyes, my vision's not as clear.
I want to feel the world with the hands that made it, know the pain and appreciate it,
Hear their cries and hope to understand.

chorus

My world view, it's how I see the world, it's how I look at you.
My world view, it's how I see the world, would you like to see it too?
My world view.

I want to place my foot upon the rock, the rock that doesn't move.
For upon the rock the Kingdom's built, and here's the Kingdom view.
I see creation and I see Adam's fall, I see through the years and I can see it all.
All things come together for the good.

chorus II

My world view, it's how I see the world, it's how I look at you.
My world view, it's how I see the world, would you like to see it too?
My world view, it's how I see the world, would you like to see it too?
My world view, coming into view, coming into view, coming into full view.

chorus III

My world view, I can see, I can see it forever.
It's how I see the world, it's how I look at you.
My world view, coming into view, coming into full view, it's how I see the world,
would you like to see it too?

genesis study

Read each of the following passages from Genesis and write in the "worldview" category or categories that relate to it.

1:1 - "In the beginning God..."

_____

1:1 - "...God created the heavens and the earth..."

_____

1:21 - "So God created the great creatures of the sea and every living and moving thing... according to its kind."

_____

2:7 - "...and man became a living soul."

_____

2:9 - "...the tree of the knowledge of good and evil."

_____

2:16 - "...the Lord God commanded the man,'...you must not eat from the tree...' "

_____

2:24 - "For this reason a man will leave his father and mother and be united to his wife..."

_____

6:9 - "This is the account of Noah..."

_____

9:6 - "Whoever sheds the blood of man, by man shall his blood be shed..."

_____

42:3 - "Then ten of Joseph's brothers went down to buy grain from Egypt."

_____

thinking like a christian

categories that make a WORLDVIEW

CATEGORY:	DEFINITION / KEY QUESTION
theology:	The study of the existence, nature, and attributes of God. **What about God?**
philosophy:	The love of wisdom: the attempt to discover an explanation for the whole of existence or reality. **What is real?**
biology:	The study of living organisms. **What about life?**
psychology:	The study of the soul, mind, and spirit. **What about human nature?**
ethics:	The study of what is right and what is wrong behavior. **What's right?**
sociology:	The study of social institutions and society. **How about relationships?**
law:	The study of the basic principles of nature and human conduct which are expected to be observed. **What are the rules?**
politics:	The art of governing a city, state, or nation. **What about government?**
economics:	The management of resources, whether by an individual or a society. **What about money?**
history:	The study of past places, persons, and events. **What about the past?**

parent up-date:

Dear Parents:

For the next twelve weeks your teen will be involved in the following course:

TITLE: WORLDVIEWS IN FOCUS: "Thinking like a Christian"

COURSE DESCRIPTION: The late Christian thinker and author, Francis Schaeffer, wrote, "The basic problem of the Christians in this country...is that they have seen things in bits and pieces instead of totals..." Thus, we need to see the "total" picture about biblical truth - that it applies to every area of our lives. Practical Christian living comes from applying biblical principles to our understanding of law, politics, biology, psychology, sociology, ethics, even why we study history. Then, like the men of the tribe of Issachar who "understood the times, with knowledge of what Israel should do..." (1 Chron. 12:32), our youth will be able to discern what they should do in our society today. Examples will be found in the daily newspaper and current movies and T.V., to show the relevance of thinking like a Christian in everyday living at home, in school, and with their friends.

MAIN TEXT: *Understanding the Times*, David A. Noebel.

This course comes with a Student JOURNAL in which there are daily assignments. Each exercise takes about 10 - 15 minutes to complete. These exercises reinforce the concepts learned during the weekly group meetings, and give additional information to enhance the scope and application of the content. Encourage your teen each day as they spend time in their JOURNAL.

Also, you will want to take every opportunity to reinforce at home the content and principles being taught in this course. For this first week, you may wish to review with your teen 1 Chronicles 12:32, and discuss the implications for your life and theirs.

Please give me a call if you have any questions or comments related to your teen and what we are studying at church.

Yours in Jesus,

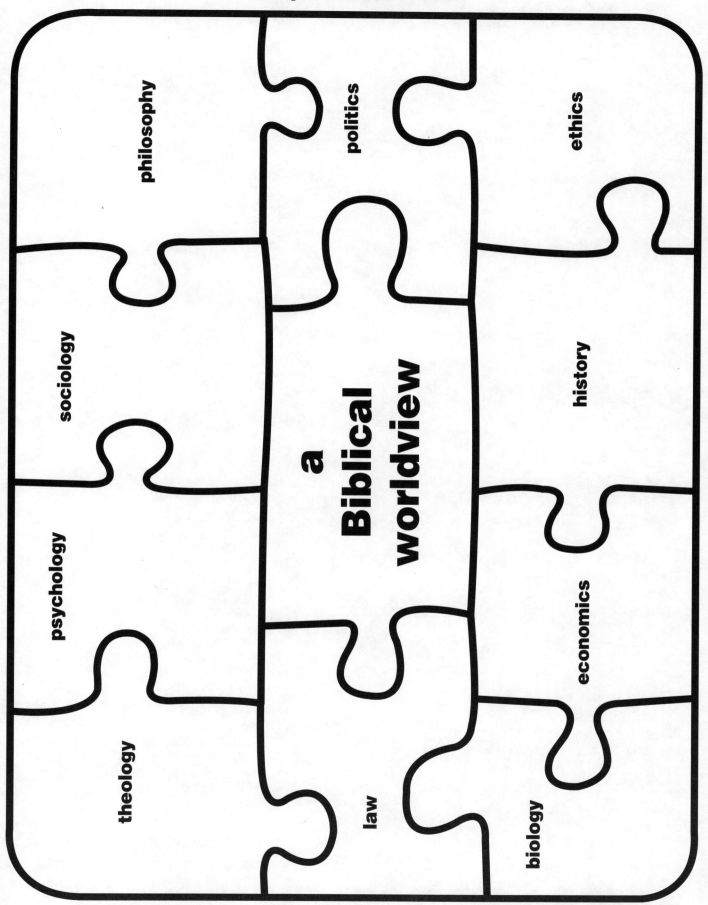

philosophy

politics

ethics

sociology

history

psychology

a
Biblical
worldview

theology

law

biology

economics

notes & ideas

lesson 2

theology: what about god?

"Is there a God?" and "What is God like?" are questions that have been debated over the years. That debate continues to this day. Yet, the essential foundation of Christianity rests on the fact that "God is!" and that He has certain attributes.

In this lesson on Theology, students will learn three important aspects of God's nature: He is the Ruler of the universe, He is Relational with mankind, and He is Righteous in all His ways. The three characteristics are simple to remember, yet they encompass all of the major attributes of God.

For example, under the concept of Ruler are the qualities of Omnipotence (all-powerful), Omnipresence (all-present), and Omniscience (all-knowledge). God's Relational dimension, encompassing His creation of mankind to be in relationship with Him, includes His love, forgiveness, and grace. The fact that God is Righteous implies that He is Holy and judges sin.

Using these three attributes of God makes it easy to show how His character is consistent. For example, God sent Jesus to become a man (Because God Rules He has the power to invade humanity.) to die for our sins (Because God is Righteous He demands payment for our sin problem.) in order to restore fellowship with those who accept His offer of forgiveness (Because God is Relational He desires our fellowship.).

In this lesson you will show how these characteristics of God make it possible to have a personal relationship with Him through Jesus Christ. Our sinful nature is discussed and related to our need for a Savior. The opportunity to receive Christ as Savior is specifically covered in Lesson #5, Biblical Psychology.

theology

key concept: Jesus is the fullness of God

key verse: Colossians 2:9
"For in Christ all the fullness of the Deity lives in bodily form."

objectives: By the end of this lesson, each student should be able to
FOR THE REVIEW SESSION: INTRODUCTION
. . . discuss why Christians have a "bit and piece" focus on Christianity.
. . . defend the idea that all areas of life are sacred.

FOR NEW TOPIC: THEOLOGY
. . . relate how the foundation of a worldview depends on the nature of God (Theology).
. . . state three important characteristics of God: He Rules, He Relates to His creation, and He is Righteous.
. . . relate those characteristics of God to his or her own relationship with God.

read: U.T.T., Chapter 6, Biblical Christian Theology.

before class:

☐ Put up the "bulletin board" idea suggested at the close of the first lesson. This will be referred to at the beginning of this lesson. It also serves as a weekly reminder of how these seemingly different ideas fit together into a unified whole. It provides a strong mental image of the biblical worldview.

☐ Study the verses on the worksheet, "What is God Like?" and be prepared to lead a discussion on how these verses relate to a characteristic of God as suggested in the teaching outline, III, B.

☐ Make copies of the three handouts, **"What is God Like?," "How God Relates To Me,"** and **"My Christian Worldview of Theology"** for each student. Have a pencil and Bible for everyone.

note:

As each student comes into class, ask if he brought an article from the newspaper. If someone does not have an article, have him pick one of the newspaper articles from last week's lesson and read it to himself while the others are coming into class. ALSO, you might want to have the Audio Adrenalin song, "My World View," playing in the background.

PART ONE: REVIEW INTRODUCTION

1. REVIEW: Ask students to briefly review the main ideas from last week's lesson. See if they can summarize the lesson in a short sentence (i.e., the Bible relates to all of life). Refer to **Colossians 2:6-9** and discuss how Jesus relates to our worldview.

2. QUESTIONS?: ASK if they have any questions from their individual study during the week. Briefly respond to questions by redirecting their questions to the group to discuss. Add your comments as a summary and move on to another question or the next point in the review session.

3. SCHAEFFER QUOTE: Mention the following quote from Schaeffer as you point to the bulletin board and review the ten categories: "The basic problem of the Christians in this country in the last eighty years or so, in regard to society and in regard to government, is that they have seen things in bits and pieces instead of totals" (UTT, p. 4). DISCUSS how this "bit and piece" focus is true for others they know and for themselves.

4. ARTICLES: Have each student share his article from the newspaper with the rest of the class. Encourage the group to discuss the placement of the article under a worldview category.

   NOTE: Again, this exercise is not an exact science. The article may relate to several areas. Lead the class to decide which is the primary category. They will get better at this as they learn more about the 10 categories. The purpose here is not to debate which area is the "best," but to promote thinking in "Christian categories." Then instruct the student to tape the article on the bulletin board in the appropriate piece of the puzzle.

5. SECULAR vs. SACRED: Remind the group of the exercise from last week where they placed articles on either side of the line marked "Relates to the Bible" and "Does not relate to the Bible." During the week in their JOURNALS they explored the issue of the difference between the "secular" and the "sacred." Relate those two exercises to show that they both were describing the same idea - that everything relates to the Bible and is sacred. Then link this idea with the biblical evidence of God's redemptive order by reading just the redemptive concept. Have the group relate that concept to one or more of the ten worldview categories on the bulletin board. Read from the paragraph beginning, "Further, God manifests Himself in the form of Christ. . ." on page 14 of UTT.

6. TRANSITION: SAY: **We've been taking a bird's eye view by getting the BIG PICTURE concerning a worldview. We will now dive down to get a worm's eye view of one of these ten categories.**

PART TWO: NEW TOPIC- THEOLOGY

I. INTRODUCTION:

A. NEW GIRL IN SCHOOL: SAY: **There is a new girl on campus. You are introduced to her in class. Since she is new, you show her the way to the cafeteria and ask if she wants to eat lunch together. As you are eating, she mentions that she is a Hindu. You respond that you are a Christian. She then asks you a question: "What is your God like?" So, what do you say?**
(Various answers.) Do not critique students' responses at this time. Allow several to voice their ideas.

1. SAY: **This question, "What is God like?" is one of the most basic questions that a person can ever ask. In fact, it forms the basis for the rest of your worldview. When you ask this question, you are dealing with which of the 10 areas?** (Theology)

2. HOUSE ILLUSTRATION: Draw a simple outline of a house on the board. Be sure to include the foundation. SAY: **Think with me about the structure of a house. What is the most important part of a house?** (The foundation) **Why?** (If it's not stable or solid, then the whole structure may fall.) **In building a house, the foundation is the first and most important part. In a similar way, when we think about building a worldview, we need to start with a firm foundation.**

B. BULLETIN BOARD PUZZLE: ASK: **Which of the ten categories do you think is foundational to the rest? Why?** (Theology, because it answers the most fundamental questions about reality and God. It forms the basis of what we call "religion.")

C. TRANSITION: **Today, we'll learn about the foundational area of "Theology." "Theology" comes from two Greek words, "theos" meaning "God" and "logos" meaning knowledge or the study of something. Theology answers the question: "Is there a God and what is God like?" In other words: "What about God?"**

II. WHAT ABOUT GOD?

A. TWO OPTIONS: Draw the following diagram on the board as you SAY: **Basically there are two ways that people have answered the question: "WHAT ABOUT GOD?" Either "GOD IS," or "GOD IS NOT."**

WHAT ABOUT GOD?

GOD IS   GOD IS NOT

People who believe "God is" are called "theists." Those who believe "God is not" are "atheists." Surveys indicate that over 90% of Americans believe in God. Less than 10% admit to being atheists, or not believing in God. As you can imagine, the way you answer this first question will affect how you view a lot of other areas.

B. HANDOUT: Give each student the handout, "What is God Like?" Have them look at the quote on the top of the sheet as you read it aloud: **"Theism, the belief that God is, and atheism, the belief that God is not, are not simply two beliefs. They are two fundamental ways of seeing the whole of existence. The one, theism, sees existence as ultimately meaningful, as having a meaning beyond itself; the other sees existence as having no meaning beyond itself."** Stephen D. Schwartz (quoted in U.T.T., p. 47.)

C. SAY: **Think about that statement for a minute. If God is at the center, or the foundation, of your worldview, how does that affect the other nine areas of knowledge? Someone choose one of the categories from the board. How does a belief in God affect what you think about that category?** (Pause for discussion.) **And what happens if God is not the foundation? Who replaces God?** (Get the students to agree that man would replace God as the center of knowledge.)

thinking like a christian

D. SAY: **Someone pick one of the other categories from our worldview puzzle on the wall, and let's discuss how a view of God relates to that area.** Select a volunteer to name a category, for example "Biology." Then ask for a volunteer to suggest how a theist would answer the question: What is the origin of life? This is the question taken from the first week's handout, "Categories that make a Worldview." Next, ask for a volunteer to suggest how an atheist might answer that same question. Then ask for another volunteer to select another category and use the handout to ask the question associated with it. Do this two or three times. You may need to prompt them if they get stuck on an answer.

NOTE: Do not get into a long discussion on any of these areas at this point. You do not have time to cover all ten categories. The rest of the course will go into more detail. The point is to reinforce the concept that one's view of God influences how one thinks about every other area.

E. SUMMARY: SAY: **As you can see, what you think about God relates to how you think about everything else in life. An atheist views the world totally differently from that of an atheist.**

F. TRANSITION: SAY: **Since our focus during this series is on the biblical view of life, we will assume that "God is." But this brings us to the second part of the question of Theology: "What is God like?"**

III. GOD'S REVELATION TO US

A. SAY: **The Bible tells us that God has chosen to reveal himself to us in two ways: Through GENERAL REVELATION and SPECIAL REVELATION. Let's consider each of these for a moment.**

NOTE: More detail will be given in the **STUDENT JOURNAL.** This section simply introduces the key ideas.

1. SAY: **GENERAL REVELATION is the created order, or the world of nature. How is God's character revealed through the created order?** (Allow students to discuss the design, the orderliness, the beauty, etc. in the world He created.)

   a. **When we look at the natural world, can we know general things about God or specific things about Him?** (General things.)

   b. **What do we need in order to find out specific things about what God is like?** (The Bible.)

2. SAY: **SPECIAL REVELATION is another term for the Bible and what it tells us about God and about Christ. The Bible claims to be from God, so that is why we say that God is revealing Himself to us not in just a general way, but in a special and specific way.**

B. TRANSITION: **So now, let's turn to the Bible to see what specific things we can learn about God and how that relates to our understanding of the world around us.**

IV. THREE CHARACTERISTICS OF GOD: SCRIPTURE SEARCH

A. DIVIDE THE CLASS INTO THREE GROUPS
Have the class stand and number off, 1-2-3. Then all "ones" move their chairs together to form group one, all "twos" create group two, all "threes" create a third group.

1. In each group, whoever's birthday is closest to January 1st is to be the "Reader." Each "Reader" is to read aloud to his group each of the passages assigned to his group. The person with a birthday closest to June 1st is to be the "Reporter." His job is to report to the rest of the class what his group has said about each verse and the overall summary of the passages.

2. After giving the groups 6 minutes to discuss their passages, have the "Reporter" give a summary of each verse and then how they completed the sentence: "God is _____. " ASK: **Are there any questions about your activity before we begin? If not, you will have 6 minutes to complete your task.**

B. THE THREE "R'S": As each group reports their findings, show them how the **suggested** three "R's" listed below **summarize** what they have read in each group. Write "Relational," "Righteous," and "Ruler" on the board under the heading "God is."

NOTE: The three "R's" are simply a general summary of the major attributes of God. These are not exhaustive; however, they do cover a wide range of characteristics that could be included in each area. The point here is not to debate the three "R's," but to suggest that these are three major areas which tell us a lot about God's character. The practical application will come under C.2.

1. **GOD IS RELATIONAL:**

   a. Genesis 1:26-28: (God created mankind in His image so that we could have a relationship with Him.)

   b. Romans 5:8: (Our relationship with God is dependent on our acceptance of Christ's work on the cross.)

   c. Matthew 22: 37-39: (The relational character of God commands us to love Him and love our neighbor as ourselves. The relationship is both vertical and horizontal.)

2. **GOD IS RIGHTEOUS:** (All three passages mention God's "Righteousness.")

   a. 2 Timothy 4:8

   b. Ezra 9:15

   c. Daniel 9:14

3. **GOD IS RULER:**

   a. Genesis 17:1: ("Almighty" means that God has the power to rule.)

   b. Jeremiah 32:17: ("Sovereign" means that God has that ability to rule.)

   c. Matthew 19:26: ("All things are possible" means that God rules over everything.)

thinking like a christian

C. DISCUSSION: Draw the students out during this next section with leading questions to make them think about the importance and implications of God's character.

1. GENERAL QUESTIONS: As they respond to the following questions, write key words or phrases on the board under the three headings of "Ruler," "Righteous," and "Relational".

   a. **How would you describe a person who is very relational, one who is good at relating to other people?** (Various answers.)

   b. **What does it mean to be righteous? How would a righteous person act in private or in public?** (Various answers.)

   c. **What is a ruler like? Think of a King. What power does he have?** (Various answers.)

2. DISCUSS "GOD IS...": **These three characteristics, "Relational, Righteous, and Ruler," as we've seen from our Bible study, are true of God. Let's think about how all three of these characteristics are important.**

   a. **What does it mean that God is Ruler?** (Various answers: He is all-powerful. He makes up the laws that rule the universe, our lives, etc.)

      (1) **What if God were ruler, but not relational?** (Various answers: He would be powerful but not care for us. He may deal with us harshly or destroy us.)

      (2) **What if God were ruler but not righteous?** (There would be no holy standards to live by. Again, He might be cruel and unjust in His dealings with us.)

   b. **What does it mean that God is Relational?** (He loves and cares for us.)

      (1) **What if God were relational but not righteous?** (Various answers: He would love us, but not care what we did. We could live as we please and not worry about what God thought.)

      (2) **Can you think of an illustration in real life that would help us picture what this would be like?** (For example, you are caught for speeding and given a ticket; but the judge does not impose a fine because he loves everybody and does not care about being just or making the right judgment.)

   c. **What does it mean that God is Righteous?** (He is perfectly Holy and Just. He always does the right thing. He demands that we live holy lives according to His laws.)

      (1) **What if God were righteous but not ruler?** (He would demand that we live holy lives, but would not be able to do anything about it if we didn't.)

      (2) **What if God were righteous but not relational?** (He would not have sent Jesus to save us from our sins.)

   d. OTHER CHARACTERISTICS: Have students shout out different qualities about God. As they relay each one, have them decide which of the three "R's" (Ruler, Relational, Righteous)

thinking like a christian

that characteristic fits. Example: God is. . . Love, Grace, Forgiving, Mercy = Relational. God is. . .Holy, Perfect, Just, Judge = Righteous. God is . . . Omnipotent, Omnipresent, Omniscient = Ruler.

3. SUMMARY: **You can see how each of these characteristics of God is important and how they combine to help our understanding of His character. Everything that is true about God can be seen in light of one of these three categories. These are easy references for understanding some things about God.**

V. APPLICATION TO REAL LIFE

A. "HOW GOD RELATES TO ME":

1. SAY: **Now let's see how God's character relates to each of us. Look on the handout "HOW GOD RELATES TO ME" and take a few minutes to individually complete the three sentences. Be as specific as possible. For example, in completing the sentence, "Because God is righteous, then, as His follower I should...," write one or more specific things you should do. Don't just write "be good." Rather, think about your life and relationships and write something like, "stop listening to music with crude lyrics."** Other examples might be "Because God is relational, I can pray to Him about my inner struggle with impure thoughts." or "Because God is righteous, I should not be watching some of the movies that I have been viewing, but instead confess that to Him." NOTE: The responses should be personalized to fit THEIR own lives. As time permits, ask volunteers if they would like to share what they have written.

2. SUMMARY: **These are some of the aspects of God's nature. You see why each of these characteristics of God is important to us and forms the foundation of our view of the world. Because God is Relational, Righteous, and Ruler. He is in charge; He loves us and demands that we live according to His standards. This is the personal God of the Bible.**

3. PARAGRAPH FILL-IN SHEET: **Using the next handout titled "My Christian Worldview of Theology," fill in the blanks as we review together the aspects we have covered in a Christian worldview of Theology.** Help the students fill in the blanks in their paragraphs. The paragraph should read: "My Christian worldview of theology states emphatically that **"God is."** I come to know Him through **special** and **general** revelation; He is the God of the **Bible.** My Christian perspective of theology also insists I must know Jesus Christ as Savior and Lord of my own life. I must have an all consuming passion for Jesus, and seek growth in the personal application of biblical teaching to every aspect of life. In the Bible, God is revealed as **Relational, Righteous,** and **Ruler.** Theology is at the **foundation** of every worldview, and **Jesus Christ** is the foundation of the Christian worldview."

B. PRAYER: **Let's close in prayer. Several of you pray out loud, each choosing one characteristic of God, thanking Him for who He is and how He relates to you.**

C. CLOSING REMARKS:

    1. NEXT WEEK: Point to the bulletin board and SAY: **In the coming weeks we will continue studying the formation of a biblical worldview. During this week, as you attend classes, watch TV or movies, or listen to CD's, think about how the things you are learning or watching fit into one of these categories. Think about what the Bible says about it; then, come report to us what you are learning about the biblical worldview and real life.**

    2. JOURNAL REMINDER: Remind students to spend some time each day in their Journals. The daily exercises will reinforce the ideas from the lesson. In this way they will be prepared to "give a defense" when they are asked about their faith.

    3. FOR HIGH SCHOOL YOUTH:
    PARENT TALK: SAY: **Review the major points of our group study with your parents. Ask them to complete the questions on the second page of the handout and share their thoughts with you.**

What is God Like?

"Theism, the belief that God is, and atheism, the belief that God is not, are not simply two beliefs. They are two fundamental ways of seeing the whole of existence. The one, theism, sees existence as ultimately meaningful, as having a meaning beyond itself; the other sees existence as having no meaning beyond itself."

- Stephen D. Schwartz (quoted in *Understanding the Times,* Abridged, p. 47.)

What does the Bible tell us about God? Embark on a Scripture search by reading each verse out loud and, as a group, decide what it says about the character of God. Write your summary beside the verse. Then, decide together on a word or phrase that would combine the ideas of the verses, and write that in the blank to describe one characteristic of God.

Group 1: God is _____:

       Genesis 1:26-28 -

       Romans 5:8 -

       Matthew 22: 37-39 -

Group 2: God is _____:

       2 Timothy. 4:8 -

       Ezra 9:15 -

       Daniel 9:14 -

Group 3: God is _____:

       Genesis 17:1 -

       Jeremiah 32:17 -

       Matthew 19:26 -

How God Relates To Me!

because God is **relational**, I can . . .

because God is **righteous**, I should . . .

because God is **ruler**, I need to . . .

SUMMARY:

"God existed as Father, Son, and Holy Spirit before His creative acts; God created the heavens and the earth; God created mankind along with the rest of his creation, and placed mankind in charge of the environment; God loved mankind in spite of man's sinful, rebellious attitude toward God; God provided a Savior in the person of Jesus Christ, who said, 'I am the way, and the truth, and the life; no one comes to the Father, but through Me' (John 14:6); and God's purpose for redeemed mankind involves a New Heaven, New Earth, and New Jerusalem--an eternity with the triune God."

- *Understanding the Times*, p. 106.

My Christian

Worldview

of Theology

My Christian worldview of theology states emphatically that "_____ ____."

I come to know Him through _____ and _____ revelation. He is the God

of the _____. My Christian perspective of theology also insists I must know

Jesus Christ as Savior and Lord of ___ _____ life. I must have an all consum-

ing passion for Jesus, and seek growth in the personal application of biblical

teachings to every aspect of life. In the Bible, God is _____,

_____, and _____. Theology is at the _____ of every

worldview, and _____ _____ is the root of the Christian worldview.

lesson 3

philosophy: what's real?

"Philosophy" can sound pretty intimidating to most students. . . and even some adults! It seems to forebode dry and boring lectures from white-haired men in dimly-lit rooms filled with musty old books. Yet, philosophy doesn't have to bore us to death. Philosophy deals with a very basic idea: "What is real and how do I know what is real?" This question has many exciting implications for the way we live everyday.

In fact, the study of philosophy should be a quest for every Christian, since Paul left us his example to "...demolish arguments and every pretension that sets itself up against the knowledge of God, and we take captive every thought to make it obedient to Christ" (2 Corinthians 10:5). Also, we are told that in Christ are hidden all the treasures of wisdom and knowledge (Colossians 2:3). As Christians, we should be true "philosophers." In the Greek language this means "lovers of wisdom."

This lesson brings the question of philosophy, or "wise living," down to a level that students can appreciate. It shows that "reality" is a topic that is very much on their minds, whether they realize it or not. For example, the reason people don't walk off the top of a tall building is that they instinctively know something about reality – we call it the law of gravity! And since gravity is part of the real world, those who seek to cooperate with that reality are living according to "wisdom."

This lesson explores the idea of **"what is real"**, and stresses the principle that "IDEAS HAVE CONSEQUENCES." This echoes the biblical principle of "sowing and reaping." The Bible makes it clear that reality consists of two realms: the natural and the supernatural. Only as students understand and live according to both realms will life have true meaning and purpose.

During their daily journal entries this week, students will answer the question "How do I now what is real?" Next week's group lesson will review this issue if you are using the 90 minute format.

While some students tend to be "wise guys," this lesson will help them understand the times and the need for truly "wise living."

lesson three

philosophy

key concept: Jesus is the Logos of God

key verses: John 1:1-2
"In the beginning was the Word, and the Word was with God, and the Word was God. The same was in the beginning with God."

objectives: By the end of this lesson, each student should be able to
FOR THE REVIEW SESSION: THEOLOGY
. . . clearly state three main characteristics of God.
. . . discuss the reasons for believing God is real.

FOR NEW TOPIC: PHILOSOPHY
. . . know why ideas have consequences.
. . . state the biblical view of reality in contrast to naturalism and spiritualism.
. . . embrace the biblical view of reality.

read: U.T.T., Chapter 10, Biblical Christian Philosophy.

before class:
FOR NEW TOPIC: PHILOSOPHY
☐ Have the three pictures (see A1, A2, & A3 at the end of this lesson) ready to show. These could be copied onto an overhead cell and projected onto the wall or screen. Otherwise, just hold up the prints one at a time for everyone to see.
☐ Bring a stove-top style coffee pot as an object lesson for III, B, 1.
☐ For III, B, 1 & 2: Ask two students to "volunteer" with a part in this lesson. Ask one student to represent the view that all of reality is spiritual and the other to represent the view that all of reality is natural. Tell them that they can try to defend their view to the rest of the class if they want to and that you will let them know when to come up in front of the class.
☐ Bring a 3 x 5 card and pencil for every student.

PART ONE: REVIEW THEOLOGY

1. ASK: **Who brought an article from the paper to share with the rest of class?** Have him summarize his article and place it on the bulletin board in the appropriate piece of the puzzle.

2. DISCUSS: **Last week we discussed "Theology." What is the main question that "theology" answers?** (Is there a God and what is God like?) **Who can summarize the lesson from last week?** (Our Christian worldview of theology says, "God is!" God reveals Himself through general and special revelation; and He is relational (personal and wants to relate to us), righteous (Holy, Just and Judge and has moral standards for our lives), and rules (He is all-powerful, Creator, and has the power to become a man and dwell among us in the person of Jesus Christ.)

3. ASK: **How does General Revelation help us know that God is real?** (Review Day 2 & 3 in the Student Journal on "Watches, Minds, and Morals.") **What is a limitation of General Revelation?** (It is not specific enough.)

4. ASK: **To which of the three "R's" (Ruler, Relational, & Righteous) does God's moral character belong and why?** (Righteous, because it is the moral standard by which we evaluate all moral decisions) You may need to remind students that "righteous" = doing the "right" thing. **How does God's righteousness affect your life?** (Because God is righteous, we should live righteous lives. Also, because God is righteous, His justice demands payment for our unrighteousness (sin), which sets the stage for Jesus's death on the cross in our place.)

5. READ AND DISCUSS: Read the following sentence out loud, one phrase at a time, and have students determine which worldview category is reflected in each phrase: **C. E. M. Joad was a seeker of truth** (Philosophy) **who was studying human nature** (Psychology) **and came to realize that men were moral creatures** (Ethics) **which led to his conclusion that there must be a God** (Theology). Discuss the worldview connections and the fact that all the pieces fit together to form a coherent whole, like the pieces of the "worldview" puzzle bulletin board.

6. ASK: **What is so special about special revelation?** (In the Bible, we learn the specifics about God's love and forgiveness through Jesus Christ.) **What does the Bible tell us about some other specific attributes of God's character?** (See Day 4 & 5 in the Student Journal: God is personal, with characteristics of love, sorrow, satisfaction, grief, anger, jealousy, etc.)

7. REVIEW: **Colossians 2:8-10:** read it aloud and point out the connection between v. 9 and 10. SAY: **Discuss the fact that Christ is the fullness of Deity and that he lives in all of us. What does that imply about our ability to live pleasing to God, resist temptation, etc.?**

8. TRANSITION: In the Colossians passage, point out the connection between v. 9 -- Christ being the fullness of Deity (Theology) and v. 8 which reflects on Christ being the foundation of Philosophy. **This introduces our session today on "Philosophy."**

I. INTRODUCTION:

    A. PERSPECTIVE PICTURES: SAY: **Perspective is very important in life. We all look at life in different ways, or from different perspectives. To test your perspective, look at each picture and tell me what it represents. Remember, it all depends on how you look at it.** Show the three pictures (A1, A2, & A3), one at a time, and with each picture ask: **What is your perspective on this picture?** Let them give various answers before you offer the following suggestions:

        1. **#1 = a six foot man asleep in a five foot tepee.**

        2. **#2 = an aerial view--you are flying overhead looking down on a man wearing a large hat** (point to the circle within a circle)... **frying an egg** (point to the first inner circle of the three circles)... **sunny-side up** (point to the "O" of the innermost of the three circles).

        3. **#3 = an aerial view of a downhill skier who failed to negotiate a tree!**

        4. SAY: **It all depends on your perspective. Each of us has different ideas about what these pictures represent. And like they say, "Ideas are like noses; everybody's got one!"**

    B. SAY: **Everybody has a different idea about life, but some ideas are better than others. In looking at these pictures, your perspective does not matter greatly, but the ideas you hold about life can matter quite a bit. You need to be certain that your perspective on the world is valid.**

    C. SAY: **This week we will continue our journey along the road to developing a biblical worldview. We begin by introducing you to philosophy. It is the second discipline we will consider in our total worldview picture.**

    D. TRANSITION: **Let's take a closer look at what it means to live in the real world.**

II. THE IMPORTANCE OF LIVING IN THE REAL WORLD

    A. DEBATE: Divide the class into two groups by drawing an imaginary line down the middle of the room. Assign the group on your left as "Group A" and the half on your right as "Group B".

        1. SAY: **Let's say that group "A" believes that people can fly like Superman and group "B" does not believe that people can fly like Superman. What would you say to try to convince the other side that your idea is right? See how many reasons your group can come up with to defend your view of reality. Select one person from your group to be the spokesperson. You have four minutes to discuss this in your groups. When you hear me clap my hands, time is up.** Listen in on each group and prod them to think creatively and deveop more reasons for their view. Don't let them stop with just the obvious. (For example, Group A could point to the fact that we see Superman and Mary Poppins flying on T.V., so it is possible for people to fly! If Group B objects on the basis that what you see on T.V. is not real, then Group B could rebut by asking how they know a man walked on the moon. That was shown on T.V., too. Maybe it was just made up!) After four minutes for group interaction, clap your hands to stop group discussion.

2. SAY: **We will first hear from Group A and then from Group B.** Have each spokesperson present their ideas in turn. Allow a short time for debate if they seem eager to debate, but don't let it drag on.

3. ASK the entire class: **How do you decide which idea is the correct view of life?** (Have somebody try it.) **The ideas we have are very important, because our belief leads to our behavior. If you were convinced that you could fly, then you would try it. You might jump off the top of a tall building such as _____** (Name a building that is a landmark near where you live.). **But you would suffer the consequences of believing something that is not true, because it does not fit the real world.**

B. TRUTH AND CONSEQUENCES GAME: Leave the class divided into two teams, but select four students, two from each team. Designate one to be score keeper and the other three to act as judges.

1. STATE: **We are going to play a game called "Truth and Consequences." Each team will have one contestant at a time stand to play. I'll say some thing that you should or should not do. The first contestant to say correctly either "Do it!" or "No way!" gets one point for your team. The person answering correctly then has 6 seconds to tell what ONE consequence might be for doing or not doing the thing I mentioned. If you give a good reason, your team receives another point. If you don't give a good consequence, the other team gets a point. The decision of the judges is final. Let's have the first contestant from each team stand up.**

2. USE the following statements or make up your own. Have a different set of contestants for each idea. The score keeper will keep a running total of the scores on the board as the game is played.

   a. **Play in traffic** (No way!)
   b. **Do your homework** (Do it!)
   c. **Eat your spinach** (Do it!)
   d. **Touch a hot stove** (No way!)
   e. **Hang out with the "wrong" crowd** (No way!)
   f. **Read your Bible** (Do it!)

3. ANNOUNCE the winners and have everyone clap for the winning team. SAY: **We see from this that life goes better for us if we understand two things: #1 the world is designed to work in a certain way, and #2, there are consequences to our ideas and actions.**

C. MAGIC JOHNSON ILLUSTRATION: (You may use a more current sports or celebrity example.)

1. SAY: **Magic Johnson had an idea about life in the area of sexuality. It was: "The more sex the better." His belief lead to certain behavior. There is only one problem with that particular idea. Do you know what that problem is?** (It does not fit the real world. It has tragic consequences! = HIV infection.) **What do we know about the real world that would have told you that Magic Johnson was living in the world of illusion?** (S.T.D.'s [Sexually Transmitted Diseases] are real.)

2. SAY: **The same is true with the idea that you can fly. In the real world, people cannot fly like Superman. So the important thing is to understand what is true about the real world and cooperate with it. Life will go better for you.**

D. SUMMARY: **So far then, we've determined two things:** Write on the board the words in ALL CAPS.

   1. BELIEF LEADS TO BEHAVIOR. **What you believe (ideas) determines how you behave (act).**

   2. BEHAVIOR HAS CONSEQUENCES. **Your behavior has natural consequences. These consequences can be either good or bad. So the point is, we want to be sure we believe ideas that are based on reality.**

III. WHAT IS REAL?

A. "PHILOSOPHY": SAY: **This raises the question: "What is reality?", or in other words, "What is the real world really like?" Look on our bulletin board and tell me which piece of the worldview puzzle deals with this issue?** (Philosophy) **When we ask that type of question, we are asking a philosophical question. Philosophy, along with Theology, are two foundational pieces of the worldview puzzle.**

   1. WRITE the words in italics on the board as you SAY: **Philosophy is made up of two Greek words: _"philio"_, meaning _"love"_, and _"sophia"_, meaning _"wisdom."_ Philosophy is the love of wisdom, the attempt to discover meaning for the whole of existence.**

   2. SAY: **The study of philosophy answers the basic question: "What is real and how do I know what is real?"**

B. THREE IDEAS: **Let's take the first part of that question. There are basically three ways that people have tried to answer the question, "What is real?"**

   1. ALL IS SPIRIT: Draw a large circle on the board and write in it the word "Spiritual" as you say: **This circle represents all of reality...everything that is. Some people have the idea that all of reality is spiritual. The physical world that we see is just an illusion. The only thing real is the spiritual, unseen dimension. This is the Hindu idea of reality. If you grew up in India, you would be taught this view. According to this idea, one day you will wake up in the spiritual realm, and this present life will have been just like a dream...not real!**

   2. ALL IS NATURE: Below the circle you just drew, draw another circle and write in it the word "Natural" as you say: **Another way of looking at reality is to believe only what you can see, taste, touch and hear is real. There is no spiritual realm to life. There is only the world of nature: molecules, amoebas, moss, mosquitoes, Michaels and Amandas** (or add the names of two of your group)**! This is called naturalism. If there is no God, then nature is all there is. This is what atheists believe.**

3. ALL IS NATURAL AND SPIRITUAL: **The Bible gives a third way of understanding reality. Let's look at some verses that give the biblical view.** Call on two students to read the following verses in turn:

    a. GENESIS 1:1: ASK: **What does this verse imply about what is real?** ("In the beginning God" = God is real. "...created the heavens and the earth" = His creation is real, and these two realities are separate.)

    b. ROMANS 1:18-22: ASK: **What can we learn about reality from this passage?** (God has revealed that certain things are true: we can learn about some of the attributes of God by studying the created world around us [recall "General Revelation" from last week]; God and the created world, i.e. nature, are separate.)

    c. ASK: **How would you draw the biblical view of reality?** Draw on the board as students offer suggestions, leading them to the following illustration as you say the script below:

    The biblical view is that reality encompasses both the spiritual and the natural. Draw the large circle around the other two circles. **The spiritual realm, including God, is not the same as the natural world. God is distinct from nature. But God is not so distant that He is totally removed from the natural realm.** Draw two straight lines connecting the two circles. **God is also involved with His creation. He has not left the world to itself.**

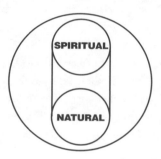

C. WHICH REALITY IS REAL? **You may have the question, "Which reality is real?" If you do, that's a good question. One way to find the answer to that question is to test the alternatives to see which one fits the real world.**

    1. NON-NATURALISM: Ask the student you contacted before class to stand.

        a. SAY: _____ (say the person's name) **is like the Hindu student last week who believes in the first view, all is spiritual and what we see in the world is just an illusion. What could you do or say to help him understand that this idea does not fit what we know about the real world?**
        Let the class wrestle with this for a minute or two and offer suggestions. Suggest that the person standing defend their belief in non-naturalism. Summarize their comments.

        b. Offer the following as a way of evaluating the idea that "all is spiritual." SAY: **What if I take a pot of boiling water and hold it over your head!** Take a coffee pot and hold it over the head of your "volunteer." **What would you do?** (Move out of the way.) **This demonstrates that you really believe that there is a physical reality. So the idea that all is spirit does not stand the "reality" test.**

        c. THANK THE STUDENT and have him sit down.

2. NATURALISM: Have the other student you contacted before class stand beside you.

    a. SAY: **Now, how about the second option, that "all is nature."** _____ (Say the person's name.) **believes that nature is all there is to reality. O.K., everyone else is going to see if they can convince you that you are wrong. Class, what would you say in this situation?** Again, allow a few minutes for debate/discussion.

    b. SAY: **Those are some good points. I want to ask you** (referring to the student standing) **a question. Do you have a mind?** (yes) **We know from observing nature that everything has a cause. So, what is the cause of your mind, the thinking processes you possess, and your unique personality? How can you account for the human mind if all is just matter? In other words, if everything is made up of just nature- molecules and electrical impulses in your brain- where did your personality and feelings of emotion come from? What in the natural world could have caused your mind?** (Pause for their answer.)

    c. SAY: **Then you have to admit that reality is more than just matter. There is an aspect to life, your mind, that cannot be accounted for in just natural terms. No neural surgeon ever cuts an idea in two! Your mind demands a cause that goes beyond matter. There must be an intelligence that is greater than the natural world and that causes the natural world to exist. Mind preceeds matter!**

    NOTE: If someone asks, "What caused God," the answer is that the law of causality states that every event has a cause. God is, by definition, "The Uncaused Cause." He is original. He is GOD. Therefore, God does not have, nor does he need to have, a cause. On the other hand, everything that we are aware of in the natural world has a cause. So the original question ("What caused your mind?") is instructive for us to contemplate.

D. SUMMARY: **Therefore, reality must 1) be real, 2) be more than just nature - that is, have a spiritual component - and 3) be understandable by the human mind. This is the way the Bible describes the world: "In the beginning, God created the heavens and the earth... " This means that God is real. Nature is real. Your mind is real. Really!**

IV. APPLICATION:

A. SCHAEFFER QUOTE: SAY: **Take a 3 X 5 card and write this on the front of it.** Write the following sentence on the board for everyone to copy. **"The truth of Christianity is that it is true to what is there." The late Francis Schaeffer wrote that in his book,** *He is There and He is Not Silent.* **We know from looking at the real world God must be there.**

B. SAY: **During the week in your JOURNAL you will see that God is not silent. He has spoken to us! You will be answering the second part of the question of "Philosophy": "How do I know what is real?"**

C. IDEAS AND BELIEFS RULE!: **One last thing. We are learning through these lessons that ideas and beliefs rule the world. The ideas you have rolling** around in your head determine what you believe and what you believe determines how you act and respond to things about you. There is a world of ideas out there that form the foundation upon which people live. Last week we learned that God rules. This week, we have learned that, as far as it concerns ourselves, "Ideas rule!"

D. WRITE A PRAYER: As we close this session, turn your card over and write a short prayer thanking God for being there for you. After a couple of minutes of writing, I'll pray out loud what I wrote. Several of you who want to can also pray out loud what you wrote. After a few minutes, close in prayer.

E. NEXT WEEK: Suggest that students explore the "World of Ideas." In order to conduct their search, they should think about the sources of information they receive every day. Look for the "ideas" behind what they study in class, or what they read in the newspaper or magazines, or what they listen to in music, and watch on T.V. or movies. As they do these things, ask them to discern the religious philosophy that is being communicated. Bring examples that they find to the next class to put on your "Worldview" puzzle. This will help build a total picture of our world and a biblical understanding of the times.

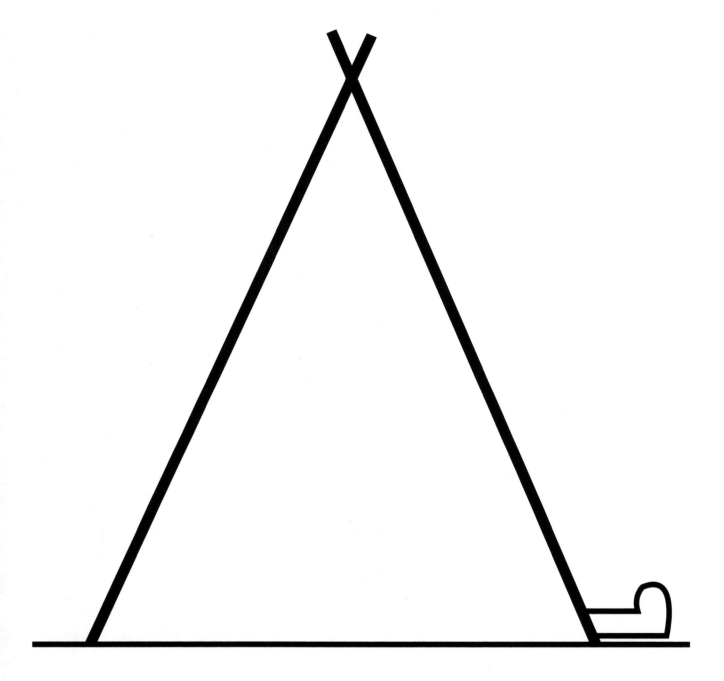

thinking like a christian

lesson 4

biology: what about life?

Related to worldviews, the field of Biology investigates the question: "What is the origin of life?" Until Darwin's publication of *The Origin of Species* in 1859, the scientific answer to that question was "God." Since Darwin, the answer from many scientists has been "mutation and natural selection plus time plus chance." Some scientists will add a few other ideas to the mix, but this is the standard Neo-Darwinian view presented in high school and college Biology textbooks.

Darwin laid the groundwork for a naturalistic explanation for the origin of life, an explanation that did not acknowledge the work of a supernatural agent (i.e. God). Today, almost all classroom textbooks present the naturalistic view, claiming that the idea of a "Creator" is a religious concept and has no place when considering "science."

The problem with the naturalistic view is that it, too, is a religious concept. The idea that the natural world is the sum total of all of reality cannot be proved by the scientific method. Most scientists today fail to recognize the religious nature of the most basic premise of evolutionary biology (i.e., that life can originate from non-living matter - something that has never been proven scientifically). Therefore, the idea of a Creator is on equal footing religiously AND scientifically with the concept of evolution.

This lesson cannot go into the details of the above debate. Our aim is to introduce students to the scientifically observable facts of the complexity of living systems. This complexity of design argues persuasively for a "Designer," which is what the Bible teaches.

If students raise additional questions outside the scope of this lesson, defer those questions and lay the groundwork according to the lesson plan. More examples and other issues, such as the fossil record, are covered in the Student Journal.

Recommended reading for additional study in "Biology": Charles Thaxton, Ph.D. in Chemistry: *The Soul of Science*, 1994; Michael J. Behe, Biochemistry Professor: *Darwin's Black Box*, 1996; Phillip E. Johnson, Law Professor: *Darwin on Trial*, 1991, and *Reason in the Balance*, 1995. You may want to subscribe to the quarterly journal, *Origins & Design*, published by Access Research Network, P.O. Box 38069, Colorado Springs, CO 80937-8069, a peer-reviewed scholarly journal, yet written on a popular level ($15/year).

> If a high-school curriculum incorporates the subject of biological origins, and if supernatural creation is a rational alternative to naturalistic evolution within that subject, then it is bad educational policy as well as viewpoint discrimination to try to keep students ignorant of an alternative that may be true.
> - Professor of Law, Phillip E. Johnson, *Reason in the Balance*, 1995, p. 26.

key concept: Jesus is the Source of Life.

key verses: John 1:3-4
"All things were made by him; and without him was not anything made that was made. In him was life; and the life was the light of men."

objectives: By the end of this lesson, each student should be able to
FOR THE REVIEW SESSION: PHILOSOPHY
. . . explain the biblical view of reality.
. . . defend the reasons for accepting the Bible as the primary source for truth.

FOR NEW TOPIC: BIOLOGY
. . . evaluate for themselves the evidence for a Creator from a biblical and scientific standpoint.
. . . reach the conclusion that the origin of life necessitates a Creator.

read: U.T.T. Chapter 18, Biblical Christian Biology.

before class:
FOR THE REVIEW SESSION: PHILOSOPHY
- [ ] Make an overhead cell of the Garfield cartoon, or an enlarged copy, so everyone can see it.
- [ ] Enlist four students to play the roles of the four people in the skit, "The Parable of Planet Boxwood." Make a copy of the skit for each person. Also, give Persons #1, #2, and #3 pieces of paper, folded to fit into their pockets, to represent the "maps" referred to in the skit.
- [ ] For each student, copy the handout, "**My Christian Worldview of Philosophy.**"

FOR NEW TOPIC: BIOLOGY
- [ ] Rehearse the opening story several times so you can tell it smoothly in class.
- [ ] For each student, have a pencil and copy of the handout, "**Biology: The Study of Life**" and "**My Christian Worldview of Biology.**"
- [ ] If possible, copy the picture of the human eye onto an overhead cell to show to the class. Other options would be to make an enlarged copy or just show it as is.
- [ ] Buy several feathers, available at most craft stores, to hand out as object lessons during the study. Have one feather for every three students.

pre-class:

As students come into the room, ask if they brought any articles from the newspaper or a magazine that relate to one of the categories of our "worldview" puzzle. If so, discuss the article with the student and have her tape it in the appropriate piece of the puzzle. As other students come in, have any student who brought in an article tell the others about it.

note:

Articles often can fit into more than one category. Help students to discern what is the most fundamental category. For example, if a man is standing trial for murdering his wife, then this involves law (the trial), sociology (family relationships), and ethics (murder is wrong). The best category to put this under is ethics, because if he had not committed murder, then the other categories would not be affected. There is room for differences of opinion on which category is best. Encouraging students to think it through is a good exercise in critical thinking.

PART ONE: REVIEW PHILOSOPHY

1. GARFIELD CARTOON: Show the Garfield cartoon. ASK: **Why is this funny?** (Various responses.) SAY: **What makes the Garfield cartoon funny is that it depicts something that is not real. The essence of humor is incongruity, or exaggeration. In the first few frames, the idea of three balls of snow falling to form a snowman stretches the imagination. But, in the last frame, Garfield's look of "Hey, what's happening here?" illustrates the fact that a little top hat floating down is totally unreal. At this point, our imagination is stretched to the breaking point and we smile in amusement at such an event. It doesn't fit the real world. We laugh at this cartoon, but it raises an interesting question: "What is real?" Obviously, we would never expect to see a top hat floating down out of the sky and landing on the head of a snowman. This is contrary to the laws of nature, to what we know to be true in the real world.**

2. WORLDVIEW PUZZLE: **Last week in our study of philosophy, we discovered what the Bible says about reality. What did we discover?** (Summarize their answers: God is real [supernatural], nature is real [natural world], and my mind is real [rationality].) You may want to redraw the illustration of the two circles within the larger circle of reality from last week's session. Point to the bulletin board puzzle piece labeled "Philosophy" and SAY: **Last week during our group session, we answered the philosophical question: "What is real?" Then during the week in your JOURNALS, you answered a second philosophical question: "How do I know what is real?"**

3. "PLANET BOXWOOD" SKIT: SAY: **To help us REVIEW that second question, I've asked four of you to help me with a short skit. It's called "The Parable of Planet Boxwood." As you know, a parable is a story that has symbolic meaning. Listen carefully to see if you can discern the meaning behind the story. We will have a short discussion after the skit.** Call the students who are participating in the skit to come to the front and read their parts. After the skit, ask the participants to remain standing while you lead the following discussion: SAY: **Let's look for some of the symbolism in this skit.**

   a. **What does the box symbolize?** (our world)

   b. **What do the three drawings of the box represent?** (different attempts to understand the world)

   c. **Person #1** (Stand beside the person who played this part.) **represents what way of understanding the world?** (personal experience or scientific investigation)

   d. **Person #2** (Stand beside the student who played this part.) **represents what way of understanding the world?** (intuition, I just try to figure it out all by myself)

   e. **Person #3** (Stand beside the student who played this part.) **represents what way of understanding the world?** (revelation, God reveals what is true about the world)

   f. **Which map would you think is the most accurate?** (map #3) **Why?** (The maker of the box would know how it was made.)

g. Thank the participants and have them sit down.

4. SUMMARY: **So to recap, there are basically three ways to answer the question: "How do I know what is real?"** Write on the board the words in **CAPS** as you give the following summary:

    a. **SCIENCE: Nature told me so. We find out about our world by studying it.**

    b. **INTUITION: I told me so. We sit around and just "think" about it. Our knowledge of the world comes from within ourselves.**

    c. **REVELATION: God told me so. Our knowledge of the world comes from outside of ourselves, from a supernatural source, i.e. God.**

5. ANOTHER QUESTION: **But this leads us to another question. Can you think of what that question might be?** (Various answers.) **There are other books that claim to be from God (i.e., the Hindu sacred writings, the Book of Mormon, etc). So the question is: How do I know that the Bible is the right source of truth?** Lead a discussion about the reasons they discovered during the week concerning why the Bible is true. (It is unique, it is reliable, and it is God-breathed.)

6. SAY: **Using the handout called, "My Christian Worldview of Philosophy," fill in the blanks as we review once more the content of our last lesson.** It should read: My Christian worldview of philosophy states that God, nature, and our minds are <u>REAL.</u> In other words, I recognize the <u>SUPERNATURAL</u> as a reality. I know what truth is, because the <u>BIBLE</u> is my source of truth. God's Word - the Bible - is <u>UNIQUE, RELIABLE,</u> and <u>GOD-BREATHED.</u>

PART TWO: NEW TOPIC - BIOLOGY

I. INTRODUCTION

    A. THE LOG CABIN STORY: Tell the "Log Cabin" story as a first person narrative in a conversational style. (See separate sheet at the end of the teaching outline for story.) You may wish to draw a log cabin on the board as you tell the story in "Chalk-Talk" style.

    B. ASK: **What do you think about my story? Do you agree with my analysis of how the log cabin came to be there? Why or why not?** (No, because structures with design do not happen through "natural" causes.) Play devil's advocate and argue your case based on the observations and facts you related in the story. Stress that you are being scientific, relying on known occurrences of energy (wind, lightening, etc.) rearranging objects. If they say that someone built it, challenge them to prove it. That's just their belief! Did they see it being built? Did they see the builder?

C. **SAY: You've probably figured out that this story is made-up. I have to admit that you have some valid points. In the real world, we all know that complex structures do not just come about by themselves, or even through simple natural causes such as lightning, wind or water. It takes an intelligent source – someone – to build a log cabin. That's just the way the real world works. And as we learned last week in discussing Philosophy, we want to understand the real world so that we will know how to live correctly.**

II. THE ORIGIN OF LIFE

A. TWO OPTIONS: **The story I just told actually leads us to think about a very important question: How did life come about? To answer that question, we enter into the study of what discipline?** (Biology) Give every student a handout, "Biology: The Study of Life," and a pencil as you SAY: **Look on our bulletin board "puzzle" and you'll notice that biology is another piece of a total worldview. Biology is the study of living things. There are basically two ways of explaining how life arrived on planet earth. These two ways relate to two terms that we introduced in our study of philosophy last week.** Write the two terms in CAPS along the top of the board as you SAY:

1. NATURALISM: **All is nature. This means that life came about through purely natural sources; life arose from non-living matter. This happened by chance mutations and blind natural selection. This view is called what?** (Evolution) As you give this definition, write on the board under the heading "Naturalism" the words: impersonal nature, life from non-life, chance ---> "evolution." Have students fill in the blanks on their handouts as you write on the board.

2. SUPERNATURALISM: **The other way of answering the question of the origin of life comes under the heading of SUPERNATURALISM. This view is that all of life came about through a supernatural, intelligent Creator acting on the natural world; life arose from prior life (i.e., a living God). Life was designed with a purpose. This view is called "Creation."** As you give this definition, under the heading "Supernaturalism" write on the board the words: Intelligent Creator, life from life, design ---> "creation."

The board should look like this:

NATURALISM	SUPERNATURALISM
impersonal nature	Intelligent Creator
life from non-life	life from life
chance ---> "evolution"	design ---> "creation"

3. WORLDVIEW PERSPECTIVE: NOTE: The following is a key point that should be stressed to the group. Go to the worldview bulletin board and point to the different pieces.

a. SAY: **You can begin to see how the pieces of the worldview puzzle are inter-related. Answering the question about the origin of life depends on your perspective about Philosophy, and that, in turn, is based on your Theology. The bottom line is, you cannot separate your Biology from your Philosophy and Theology; in other words, your "religion." They**

thinking like a christian

are linked. **Do you see that both the idea of creation and the idea of evolution are built on a RELIGIOUS FOUNDATION?** Pause to make sure this is clear. Briefly answer any questions.

   b. SAY: **Ultimately, the way you answer this question and every other question about life rests on a religious foundation. This is very important to understand. As we move through this series of lessons, this point will be made again and again. The pieces of the worldview puzzle all fit together to produce our understanding of life! Do you have any questions so far?** Briefly answer any questions related to how religion corresponds to biology. If they ask questions dealing with other issues, tell students that those issues will be addressed in later sessions, or you can discuss it at another time outside of class, or give them a book to read that deals with their question.

B. WHICH IS TRUE? **Take another look on the board at the two ways to answer the question: "What is the origin of life?" Which of these two alternatives do you think is true?** (Most students will say "creation.") **Why did you pick that one?** (Most students will probably say because the Bible says so. Acknowledge their answers and move on to the next section.)

C. EXPLAIN: **This week we will explore the origin of life from the supernatural perspective. That is the biblical view. We'll investigate two lines of evidence: God's Word and God's world.**

III. EVIDENCE FROM GOD'S WORD

A. PSALM 19 STUDY: SAY: **God's Word says that nature reveals something about God. On your handouts, take 4 minutes to answer the three questions based on the passage from Psalm 19:1-4.**

B. REVIEW: After 4 minutes review each question in turn by asking several in the group to share their answers. Suggested answers are listed on the "Teachers Copy" of the handout.

C. SAY: **But the Bible also says: "... Always be prepared to give an answer to everyone who asks you to give the reason for the hope that you have. But do this with gentleness and respect..." 1 Peter 3:15** Have students fill in the blanks as you read the verse.

   1. SAY: **Just to say, "The Bible says it, I believe it, and that settles it," may not be a sufficient answer for some people. Even though we looked at a number of reasons last week for the inspiration of the Bible, some people still want to see evidence that God is real.**

   2. EXAMPLES: **Two weeks ago we learned about General Revelation. If you recall, that is nature revealing things to us about God. Psalm 19 says that nature tells us about God. Romans 1 also says nature reveals the wisdom and power of God. On your handout, list some of the reasons, besides the Bible and the other reasons we have already studied, for believing that God created life. In what other ways does nature tell about the Creator? In other words, what specific examples from the living world attest to the fact that there must be a Creator God? Take 3 minutes to write out your reasons.**

3. SHARE ANSWERS: After 3 minutes, ask several students to share what they wrote. The point here is to get them thinking, not to have a discussion about what they wrote. Acknowledge their reasons and then move on to the next section.

IV. EVIDENCE FROM GOD'S WORLD

A. DESIGN IN THE REAL WORLD: Now let's turn our attention to the world of living things, to see what we can observe in nature that gives evidence for a Creator. We noted in an earlier session that we see "design" in the natural world. Let's look at some specific examples of design.

1. THE EYE: Show the picture of the human eye.

   a. BRAINSTORM #1: In groups of three, brainstorm together and list as many things as you can that have to work together in order for the eye to function. You have two minutes to make your list.

   b. SHARE LIST: After two minutes have each group share their list with the others. See the article at the end of this lesson for a detail of the complex inter-connections that must work together for the eye to function. Mention any that they do not list.

   c. SAY: We sometimes fail to appreciate the complexity of a common part of our own bodies. We would never assume that something of this complexity could come about by just natural processes. It takes intelligence to produce this type of system. Therefore, based on what we know about the real world, the most scientific thing we can say about the origin of the eye is that God created it!

2. A FEATHER: Give a feather to each group of three, or show the picture of a feather.

   a. SAY: Look closely at this feather. If you pull on the barbs slightly, they stay together; but if you pull harder they come apart. Now press them back together, and they hold again. It's the original "Velcro"! Each barb has a hook that intersects with an inverted hook on the barb next to it.

   b. ASK: Evolutionary scientists say that this feather developed from the scales of a reptile. Can you think of any natural process that would develop feathers from scales? (This can be either a rhetorical question or let them respond. Then ask if their scenario has any scientific basis in fact, or is it just a made-up story!) THERE IS NONE! Just like the log cabin, this type of complex structure can be made only by an Intelligent source. (For your background information, a few paragraphs on the feather are included on a separate sheet.)

3. YOUR EXAMPLE:

   a. BRAINSTORM #2: In your groups of three, brainstorm again and come up with another example to demonstrate design in nature. It could be a plant or animal or even a part of a plant or animal such as the human eye or a bird's feather. Write out the details that show the complexity of your example. Don't just say: "a fish." What is it about a fish that is

thinking like a christian

evidence of a special design and could not possibly come about through chance processes? Take five minutes to work in your groups. Circulate around the groups and help them by asking leading questions. Get them to dig deeper for details and specifics about the complex inter-workings of whatever they are considering. For example, fish have special eyes for seeing under water, gills for breathing in water, a mucus secretion over their body to help them glide through water, fins for swimming, etc.

b. SHARE IDEAS: After five minutes, have each group share their ideas with the others.

B. CONCLUSION: SAY: There are some specific things that we can conclude based on our detailed observations of the natural world. Think with me about the story I told at the beginning of class.

1. ASK: Which is the more reasonable explanation for how the house was built: by chance or by design? (By design.)

2. ASK: Now think about the specific examples we discussed: Which is the more reasonable explanation for the human eye: chance or design? (By design.) Which is the more reasonable explanation for the bird's feather: chance or design? (By design.) Which is the more reasonable explanation for _____ (select some of their examples): chance or design? (By Design)

3. ASK: When you look at our world of living systems, from people to pandas, which of the two ways of looking at the world is the more reasonable explanation for how life came about: "chance" or "design"? (Design.) Why? (Because there is no known way for a designed system to come about apart from an intelligent being acting on nature.)

4. READ the quote from the handout:

a. "The more I study science the more I am impressed with the thought that this world and universe have a definite design--and a design suggests a designer. It may be possible to have design without a designer, a picture without an artist, but my mind is unable to conceive of such a situation." - Paul Amos Moody. NOTE: The point here is not to discuss "Who is Paul Moody?". The point is the illustration he gives. Can you conceive of a picture being painted without an artist? Then there must be an artist, and there must be a Creator! All the evidence points to that logical conclusion. You can arrive at no other answer.

b. SAY: More and more scientists are coming to this same conclusion. In the past 10 to 15 years, many books have been written by university professors and scientists that attest to the fact that nature is clear in presenting evidence for a Designer! This information has not found its way into the majority of your biology textbooks. That's why we are presenting it to you here. You are free to share these ideas with your classmates and science teachers.

thinking like a christian

V. APPLY IT!

    A.   PARAGRAPH FOR BIOLOGY: Using the handout titled: **"My Christian Worldview of Biology,"** fill in the blanks with the class. The paragraph should read:

        My Christian worldview of biology declares that God is the **Creator** and **Designer** of the universe. Observing the natural world reveals an intricate and intelligent design, such as the **human eye** and a **bird's feather.** Design demands a Designer. God is the Designer." (*Students may add other examples to the list.)

    B.   PSALM OF PRAISE: Direct students to the "Apply it!" section on their handout. Suggest that they take 3-4 minutes to write a psalm praising God for His creation.

    C.   CLOSING PRAYER: Ask for 2 or 3 volunteers to read the psalm they wrote, as a part of your closing prayer.

    D.   FOR NEXT WEEK: Remind students to continue their search for the **"World of Ideas."** The ideas that underlie the things they see around them. Have them bring examples of how the Bible relates to ideas found in magazines, newspapers, and their class textbooks, especially if they are taking Biology. They may also bring examples of things that oppose the biblical worldview and discuss how these things contradict the truth as found in God's world.

    E.   FOR HIGH SCHOOL YOUTH: CLOSING REMARK: Suggest that each student take time around the dinner table to tell their family what they learned today, and share their psalm for a family devotion tonight.

thinking like a christian

why is this funny?

"the parable of planet boxwood"

NARRATOR: Once upon a time there was a world called "Planet Boxwood." It was called that because this world was shaped like a gigantic box. As you might imagine, the people who lived there were called "Boxers." One day one of the Boxers became curious about the shape of his world, so he decided to draw a map of the box in which he lived. He gathered a tape measure, a pencil, and paper, and began the laborious task of measuring and drawing "Planet Boxwood." After several years of work, he completed his map. In his excitement, he went to one of his friends to show him the fruit of his labor.

PERSON #1: "I've discovered the shape of our world! Look at the map I've drawn of "Planet Boxwood."

NARRATOR: To his amazement, his friend reached into his back pocket and pulled out a map.

PERSON #2: "Oh, really. Well I have a map, too. I drew it just the other day. I was sitting under a big oak tree and just started thinking about what our world must look like. The more I thought about it, the more things started to make sense. Finally, I put my ideas on paper. Here's my drawing."

NARRATOR: As the two compared maps, they saw a number of similarities, but also some differences. As they were comparing their maps, a third person came by.

PERSON #3: "What 'chu guys doin'?"

PERSON #1: "We're comparing maps of Planet Boxwood. Want to see what our worlds looks like?"

PERSON #3: "Sure. Let's see 'em. (Look over the maps for a few seconds, then pull out your own map.) Guess what?"

PERSON #1, #2 IN UNISON: "We know, you have a map, too!"

PERSON #3: "You're right. How'd ya guess?"

PERSON #1: "It wasn't too hard."

PERSON #3: "Well, anyway, I'd like to show ya my map. I think it should be more accurate than all of yours."

PERSON #2: "Why do you say that?"

PERSON #3: "'cause I didn't get it by taking my own measurements, or even by just thinkin' about it. I received it from the Maker of Planet Boxwood. This map shows how He designed it." (Show map to the other two as you all walk off together.)

NARRATOR: As the three Boxers looked at each of their maps, they walked off into the sunset contemplating the shape of their world.

My Christian

wor dview

of Philosophy

My Christian worldview of philosophy states that God, nature, and our minds are _____. In other

words, I recognize the _____ as a reality. I know what truth is because the _____ is my source

of truth. God's Word, the Bible, is _____, _____, and _____.

the log cabin story

"I was walking in the woods this past summer and came into a clearing. I was surprised to see a log cabin with a stone fireplace because the forest ranger had told me that this whole area was uninhabited. Being curious, I went closer to study the structure. I began to think about how the cabin must have gotten there.

Since the bark was no longer on the large logs that formed the walls, I figured there must have been a huge bolt of lightning that hit the area to strip all those logs of their bark. I've heard of lightning doing that to trees. In fact, where I used to live, we had a large tree in our front yard that was hit by lightning one afternoon while I was sitting in the living room. I went out after the storm and saw a lot of bark on the ground where the force of the electricity had literally blown it into the neighbor's yard.

Once the logs had been debarked, a strong wind must have come down off the mountain and blown over the trees. I've seen wind like that in Texas; a blue Northe'r they call it. Since the trees had started to die, due to their bark being blown off, they would have uprooted more easily and come to rest on top of each other to resemble the shape of a house.

Next, I surveyed the stone fireplace. Every stone was fitted so well that there was no need for any mortar between the rocks. At first this was hard to figure out, but then I noticed that there was a river bed close by with similar rocks all along it. A big flood must have swept through and deposited the stones into this one place. The water action would have sorted the stones until they were fitted together and then lodged there when they came upon the log structure.

Satisfied that I had explained how the cabin had come to be there, I resumed my walk through the woods."

The **human** Eye

For the human eye to function, a number of interconnecting systems have to be working in unison, including the nervous, vascular, skeletal, muscular, and endocrine systems. Two bony orbits house the globe of the eye. The bone has the appropriate holes to allow the blood vessels and nerves to feed the eye. The various layers of the eye are composed of the fibrous capsule; the sclera; the choroid; and the inner, light-sensitive retina layer. The retina contains special rod and cone neurons, bipolar neurons, and ganglion neurons, which are connected to the optic nerve, which in turn is connected to the sight center in the brain, which is connected to the grey matter, brain stem, and spinal cord for conscious awareness and reflexes.

Adding to this complex arrangement there is the lens, vitreous humor, aqueous humor, iris, ciliary body, canal of Schlemm, suspensory ligament, cornea, the lacrimal glands and ducts draining the nose, the rectus and oblique muscles for eye movement, the eyelids, lashes and eyebrows. Each of the special features of the eye is under the control of many genes. Each gene consists of thousands of nucleotides. All of these structures must be perfectly integrated and balanced with all other systems, and functioning near perfect, for the vision we depend upon to result.

(The above description of the eye is adapted from *The Creation-Evolution Controversy,* by R. L. Wysong, self published, 1976, p. 306)

The **bird's** Feather

"The flight feather of a bird is one of the most beautiful and well known of all biological adaptations. Each feather consists of a central shaft carrying a series of barbs which are positioned at right angles to the shaft to form the vane. The barbs which make up the vane are held together by rows of barbules. From the anterior barbules, hooks project downward and these interlock with ridges on the posterior barbules. Altogether, in the flight feather of a large bird, about a million barbules cooperate to bind the barbs into an impervious vane....

The use of feathers also provides the bird with an aerofoil of variable geometry so that it has the ability to vary the shape and aerodynamic properties of its wing at take-off, landing, and for various different sorts of flight - flapping, gliding, soaring. In many birds, the positioning of the feathers is maintained by an intricate system of tendons which allow the feathers to twist in such a way that when the wing is raised they open like the vanes of a blind, greatly reducing resistance, but close completely on the downstroke, thus greatly improving the efficiency of flight."

(From *Evolution: A Theory in Crisis,* Michael Denton, pp. 202-209.)

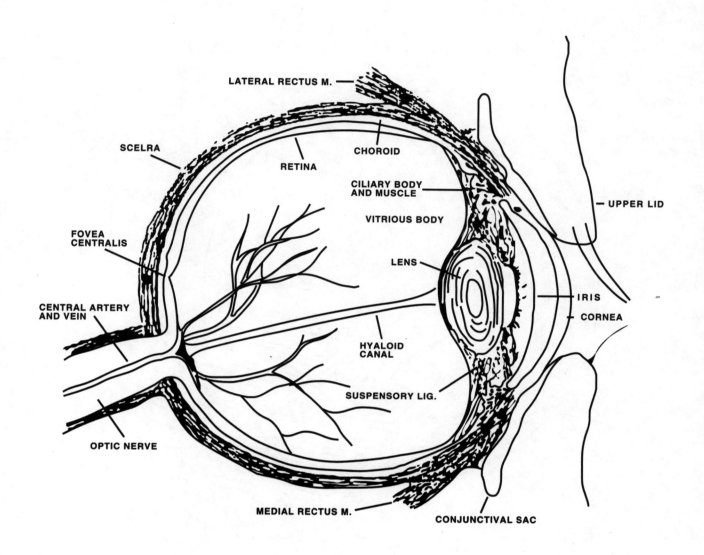

LATERAL RECTUS M. —

SCELRA

RETINA

CHOROID

CILIARY BODY
AND MUSCLE

VITRIOUS BODY

UPPER LID

FOVEA
CENTRALIS

LENS

CENTRAL ARTERY
AND VEIN

IRIS

CORNEA

HYALOID
CANAL

SUSPENSORY LIG.

OPTIC NERVE

MEDIAL RECTUS M.

CONJUNCTIVAL SAC

thinking like a christian

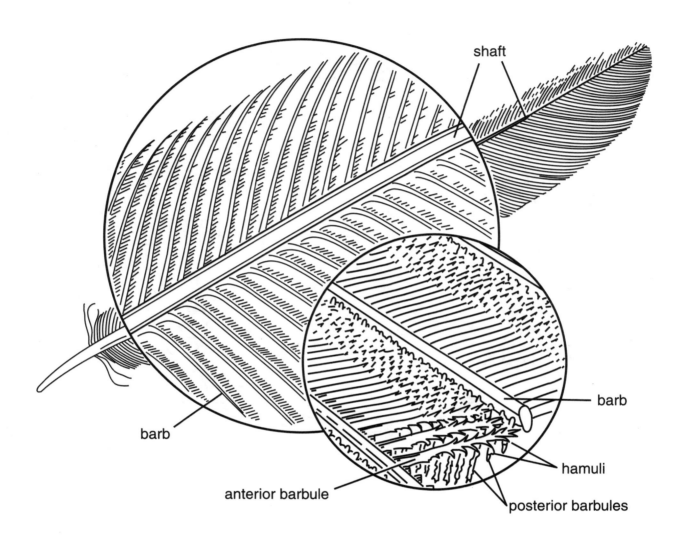

shaft

barb

barb

hamuli

anterior barbule

posterior barbules

My Christian
Worldview
of Biology

My Christian worldview of biology declares that God is the_____and _____ of

the universe. Observing the natural world reveals an intricate and intelligent design, such are the

_____ _____ and a _____ _____.

Design demands a Designer. God is that Designer.

biology: the study of life

TWO WAYS of explaining the origin of life:

naturalism

impersonal nature
life from non-life
chance ---> "evolution"

supernaturalism

Intelligent Creator
life from life
design ---> "creation"

EXPLORING GOD'S WORD:

PSALM 19:1-4

**"1 The heavens declare the glory of God; the skies proclaim the work of his hands.
2 Day after day they pour forth speech; night after night they display knowledge.
3 There is no speech or language where their voice is not heard. 4 Their voice goes
out into all the earth, their words to the ends of the world...."**

1. Verse 1: What role does the physical universe play? (It makes known to us the nature [glory] of God.)

2. Verse 2: The word "they" refers to what? (The heavens, meaning by extension, all of the natural
    realm, the cosmos, the world, every living thing.) What is it that nature pours forth and displays?
    (Speech; i.e., it is saying something about God. It gives us knowledge about God.)

3. Verses 3 - 4: Is this knowledge of God communicated to people everywhere? (yes) In what way is it
    communicated? (The "voice" of nature can be understood in every language. All people can observe
    nature and understand that it points to a Creator.)

THE BIBLE ALSO SAYS . . .

**"... Always be prepared to give an answer to everyone who asks you to give
the reason for the hope that you have. But do this with gentleness and
respect..."**

- 1 Peter 3:15

LIST THE EVIDENCES THAT CAUSE YOU TO BELIEVE GOD IS THE CREATOR.

exploring God's world:
evidence for design in nature . . .

1) The human EYE:

2) The bird's FEATHER:

3) YOUR EXAMPLE:

CONCLUSION:

The more I study science the more I am impressed with the thought that this world and universe have a definite design--and a design suggests a designer. It may be possible to have design without a designer, a picture without an artist, but my mind is unable to conceive of such a situation.
    - Paul Amos Moody, *Introduction to Evolution,* (New York: Harper and Row, 1970), pp. 497-8.

APPLY IT!
As you consider God's eternal power and divine attributes revealed through nature, in the box below write a short psalm praising God for His creation.

```



```

share it!   Share your psalm with your family or a close friend.

thinking like a christian

biology: the study of life

TWO WAYS of explaining the origin of life:

naturalism   ### supernaturalism

_____ nature   Intelligent _____

life from _____   life from _____

_____ ---> "evolution"   _____ ---> "creation"

EXPLORING GOD'S WORD:

PSALM 19:1-4
**"1 The heavens declare the glory of God; the skies proclaim the work of his hands.
2 Day after day they pour forth speech; night after night they display knowledge.
3 There is no speech or language where their voice is not heard. 4 Their voice goes
out into all the earth, their words to the ends of the world...."**

1.   Verse 1: What role does the physical universe play?

2.   Verse 2: The word "they" refers to what?

        What is it that nature pours forth and displays?

3.   Verses 3 - 4: Is this knowledge of God communicated to people everywhere?

        In what way is it communicated?

THE BIBLE ALSO SAYS . . .
        **"... Always be prepared to give an _____ to everyone who asks you to give
        the _____ for the hope that you have. But do this with gentleness and
        respect..."**

                                                        - 1 Peter 3:15

LIST THE EVIDENCES THAT CAUSE YOU TO BELIEVE GOD IS THE CREATOR.

exploring God's world:
evidence for design in nature . . .

1) The human EYE:

2) The bird's FEATHER:

3) YOUR EXAMPLE:

CONCLUSION:

The more I study science the more I am impressed with the thought that this world and universe have a definite design--and a design suggests a designer. It may be possible to have design without a designer, a picture without an artist, but my mind is unable to conceive of such a situation.

- Paul Amos Moody, *Introduction to Evolution,* (New York: Harper and Row, 1970), pp. 497-8.

APPLY IT!

As you consider God's eternal power and divine attributes revealed through nature, in the box below write a short psalm praising God for His creation.

```




```

share it! Share your psalm with your family or a close friend.

notes & ideas

lesson 5

psychology: what about human nature?

This week's topic of "psychology" at first may seem too complicated for a one-week Bible study. Psychology is usually taught as an entire college level course. Yet, the genius of Noebel's book is the ability to simplify a topic without making it "simplistic." This week's topic is no exception.

The study of the "soul" has been the stuff of theological, philosophical and psychological debate from the dawn of time. The quest to know who we are and what makes us "tick" is an ongoing dialogue. Today's culture tends to view man as basically "good," or at worst, "neutral." In either case, society shapes the individual into the kind of person he becomes, whether good or bad. This concept minimizes personal responsibility for one's actions.

The Bible gives us a unique perspective, different from the current popular view. The biblical view is that man is neither basically "good" nor basically "bad"; the biblical view of man is that he is basically "sinful." Being sinful does not mean that we are as bad as we could be; it means that we are not as good as we ought to be. In God's perspective that makes us unacceptable.

As this lesson will illustrate, our nature is actually a double exposure: made in God's image, yet totally fallen into sin. The dual aspect of our basic make-up accounts for what we actually observe in the world around us: the good and the evil deeds done by man.

Also, this lesson will help students come to grips with their own sin and understand their own need for a Savior. Depending on your knowledge of the spiritual condition of your group, the lesson offers two options for how to handle the "invitation" for individuals to trust in Christ's solution for their sin problem.

The STUDENT JOURNAL assignments deal with the topics of "self-esteem," the Christian's spiritual heritage, and making a personal commitment to live in the power of God's Spirit.

lesson five

key concept: Jesus is the Savior

key verse: I Thessalonians 5:23
"May God himself, the God of peace, sanctify you through and through. May your whole spirit, soul and body be kept blameless at the coming of our Lord Jesus Christ."

objectives: By the end of this lesson, each student should be able to

FOR THE REVIEW SESSION: BIOLOGY
. . . articulate the connection between Christianity and modern science.
. . . describe the theological implications of evolution.

FOR NEW TOPIC: PSYCHOLOGY
. . . understand that human nature is a "double exposure" (God's image + sinful) and what the Bible means by the term "sin."
. . . be challenged to accept God's solution for his sin problem (forgiveness in Christ).

read: U.T.T., Chapter 22, Biblical Christian Psychology.

before class:

FOR THE REVIEW SESSION: BIOLOGY
☐ Make an overhead cell of Pascal's "wager" or write it on the board for the discussion.

FOR NEW TOPIC: PSYCHOLOGY
For the opening "Game Show" you will need to do the following:
☐ Purchase a bag of pretzels for the prize.
☐ Have a bell, whistle or kitchen timer to get their attention.
☐ On a sheet of paper write: "Describe the basic nature of the person sitting next to you," fold it and seal it in an envelope. Write on the outside of the envelope: "THE QUESTION."
☐ On a half sheet of poster board, write in large bold letters: "APPLAUSE."
☐ Have a pencil and 3 X 5 card for each student.
☐ Bring a camera as an object lesson for II, B.
☐ Have enough Bibles for each group of three to have at least one Bible.
☐ If possible, obtain a copy of the song, "God," by Rebecca St. James, to play during class.

PART ONE: REVIEW BIOLOGY

1. THE WORLD OF IDEAS: As students come in, ask if they came across any examples from the "World of Ideas" this past week. Have them read their articles or cartoons and tape them in the appropriate piece of the worldview puzzle. Talk with them about their examples and share any articles or cartoons you came across that relate to Theology, Philosophy, or Biology. Save your articles pertaining to the other categories (Psychology, Ethics, etc.) for the appropriate lesson.

2. SAY: **Last week we covered "Biology."** ASK: **What worldview question does the study of biology answer?** (What is the origin of life?) **What is the Biblical Christian answer to that question?** ("In the beginning God created...")

3. ASK: **What difference does it make if evolution is true?** (Draw out their answers based on the quote from UTT, p. 152 beginning "More important, if evolution is true, then the story of the Garden of Eden and original sin must be viewed as nothing more than allegory, a view that undermines the significance of Christ's sinless life and sacrificial death on the cross...")

4. ASK: **What is the connection between religion and science?** (Demonstrate to the group that science does not happen in a vacuum. How you approach biology always is built upon how you view reality [philosophy] and that, in turn, is based on how you view God [theology]. You cannot separate science and religion. Either science is based on the personal God of the Bible, or on the religion of atheism, or on some other religions presupposition. Either "In the beginning God..." or "In the beginning matter...", and all else follows.)

5. DISCUSS the following questions from Day 2 in the JOURNAL:

    a. **Why was modern science not begun in other cultures or religions?** (Some religions view the universe as being indwelt by many gods [called "polytheism" as practiced by the Greeks and Romans, and the Hindu religion]. These religions teach that the world is animated by different deities. The world is not run by set laws of nature but by the whims of the deities. Therefore, there was no reason for man to investigate the laws of the natural world. Instead of looking for laws in nature, they sought to do things that would appease the various gods of the rain and sun and crops and childbirth. Other religions see god as being a part of the universe [referred to as "pantheism", such as Zen Buddhism and current day "New Age" thinking]. In this view, since everything is a part of god, the rocks, trees, dolphins, etc., then to experiment with nature is to experiment with god. People who believe this way do not try to change nature through technology.)

    b. **What does this say about the religious foundation of modern science?** (It is not based on these other worldviews, but on Biblical Christianity. While other civilizations in the past developed great technical expertise - Egypt with its pyramids, Rome with its aqueducts - only one civilization produced the experimental method we call science. That civilization was Europe at the end of the Middle Ages, a culture steeped in Christian faith.)

    c. **What is it about Christianity that would form the basis on which to study and understand the world of nature?** (First: God is described as the Creator of the universe; therefore we can study His creation and discover the order and laws that He designed. Once these laws are understood, we can convert that knowledge, through technology, to make life easier for ourselves. For example, by understanding the properties of certain metals and the laws of chemistry related to the combustibility of gas, men designed the internal combustion engine which runs our vehicles. Second: Since God made the world, we have a biblical obligation to study it and use it to the glory of God and the benefit of mankind. See Genesis 1:28 - "God blessed them and said to them, 'Be fruitful and increase in number; fill the earth and sub due it. Rule over the fish of the sea and the birds of the air and over every living creature that moves on the ground.'")

6. TRANSITION: **Now that we have seen the importance of God's involvement in creation, we will move on to see how mankind plays a special role in God's creative plan.** Hand out copies of the song, "God," by Rebecca St. James. Have students follow the words as you play the song. Then lead the following discussion:

a. ASK: **In the first stanza, Rebecca makes a connection between what two things?** (God's creative power in designing the universe and giving us life. Point out that this connects the study of Biology with Psychology.)

b. ASK: **In the second stanza, she describes people as having a "void" in their souls. What evidence of that void do you see in our world today?** (Loneliness, crime, suicide, anger, etc. Relate these or other similar things to any of the articles that are posted on the board or other current events in the news. You could spend a little time discussing these issues.)

c. SAY: **The Bible says that God has created man a "little lower than the angels and crowned him with glory and honor." (Psalm 8:5) This raises the question of "Who am I?" This session we will explore that question.**

PART TWO: NEW TOPIC - PSYCHOLOGY

I INTRODUCTION:

A. GAME SHOW: Give each student a 3 X 5 card and pencil as you SAY WITH ENTHUSIASM!: **I want to welcome you to the new game show, "Know Your Neighbor!"** Hold up "APPLAUSE" sign for a few seconds, then put it down. **Today, each of you will have the chance to be a contestant and win a big prize to share with your friends: Today's big prize is this BAG OF PRETZELS!**

1. GAME RULES: **The object of the game is to see how well you know your neighbor. To play the game, each of you should take a 3 X 5 card and a pencil, and write down a description of the person sitting to your left.** (This assumes everyone is sitting in a circle. If they are in a line or rows, have the last person in the row write about the first person on that row.) **You have one minute to list everything you can about the person sitting on your left.**

2. QUESTIONS?: **Any questions before we begin?** (How do I win the prize?) If they don't ask, tell them anyway. **That's a good question. The way to win the special prize is to give the answer to the question in this sealed envelope!** Display the envelope. **The question asks you to say something specific about the person sitting next to you. If you list the quality asked for in the envelope, you are the winner. In case of a tie, the bag of pretzels will be split among the winners. So list as many qualities of the person to your left as you can. You have one minute to make your list. When you hear the bell, stop writing. Ready? Begin now.**

3. READ THEIR CARDS: After one minute, ring a bell/blow a whistle to get everyone's attention and SAY: **O.K., time is up. Each of you will now read what you wrote down.** Start with the first person and ask him to read from his card. NOTE: Do not acknowledge at this time if he answered the "secret" question in the envelope. Do not make any comments, but go on to the next person until everyone has read his card.

4. DECLARE THE WINNER: Open the sealed envelope and read the question out loud: **"Describe the basic nature of the person sitting next to you."** Ask if anyone answered that question on their card. If so, declare the winner(s) and present the prize. Show "APPLAUSE" sign and have everyone clap as you declare the winner(s). If there is no winner, then you keep the prize, but be generous and share it with the whole class! SAY: **That's it for this week's show. Tune in next week when we will ask the question, "How do they get that twist in a pretzel, anyway?"** Show "APPLAUSE" sign.

NOTE: A person's "basic nature" goes beyond his personality or his looks. This question requires an answer on a more fundamental level, the level of the spirit. The rest of this lesson gives the answer to that question. The answer is twofold: "made in God's image and sinful." If someone gets half of the answer, count them as a winner. If no one answers the question, don't tell the class yet or it will spoil the lesson.

5. RECAP THE DIFFERENCES: **Did you notice that there is a lot of variety in what you wrote about each other? Tall, short, lean and mean, we are all quite different.**

B. THE SIMILARITY: **However, there is one major similarity among you all. In fact, every human being has something in common with all the rest of humanity. Do you know what that is?** (The spiritual nature.) If they do not get the right answer, SAY: **It relates to the question in the envelope. Right, our basic nature!**

II. HUMAN NATURE

A. BASIC NATURE: **The thing that is common to everyone is his or her basic human nature. The basic nature of someone is what he is like on a fundamental level, the thing that does not change from person to person, the aspect of humanity that is the same for all people throughout all time. All people have a basic nature. A person's basic nature goes deeper than his appearance or even his personality. It involves the very core of his being, specifically his spiritual condition.**

B. TWO PARTS OF PEOPLE: SAY: **Let's illustrate it this way.** Draw on the board a picture of a balloon person as you explain the following. See the drawing at the end of this lesson for an example.

1. PHYSICAL: Write the word "Body" beside the person as you SAY: **On the physical level, people are different. All bodies do not look alike. Some are tall, others are "vertically challenged"! There are different shapes and sizes.**

2.   SOUL: Write the word "Soul" beside the person as you SAY: **The non-physical aspect of the human being is the deepest and most basic. When we speak of this part of an individual, we are talking about the "soul."**

    a.   SAY: **"Soul" comes from a Greek word: "psyche."** Write "psyche" on the board.

    b.   ASK: **What do you call it when you study the psyche?** (Psychology.)
On the board, change the word "psyche" to "psychology" as you SAY: **So originally, "psychology" meant the study of the soul or inner part of a person.**

3.   TRANSITION: **As we continue our study of a biblical worldview, notice on our bulletin board puzzle that "Psychology" is one of the pieces that fits into the total picture. Today, we'll see how the Bible answers the question, "What is human nature?"**

III. BIBLICAL PSYCHOLOGY

A.   BIBLE DISCOVERY: Divide the class into two sides and designate those on your left as "Side A" and everyone on your right as "Side B." Then divide each side into groups of three (TRIADS). Make the following assignments:

1.   SIDE "A": "GOD'S IMAGE": On the left-hand side of the room, assign each triad to read the following passages. Write on the board the following references [Do not write out what is written in brackets; that is for your reference as the teacher.]:

    a.   Genesis 1:27-31: [man created in "God's image"]

    b.   Ecclesiastes 7:29: ["God made man upright"]

    c.   Psalm 8:3-8: [man made lower than angels & crowned with glory and honor]

2.   SIDE "B": "MAN'S SIN": On the right-hand side of the room, assign each triad the following passages. Write on the board the following passages:

    a.   Genesis 3:9-13: [Adam's disobedience]

    b.   Romans 3:23: ["all have sinned"]

    c.   Ephesians 2:1-3: [refers to "sinful nature"]

3. SAY: **You will have 5 minutes to look up and read your assigned passages from the Bible. Then, in your groups of three, summarize what the Bible passages say concerning the basic nature of man.** Circulate around the room and help groups stay on task.

4. SAY: **What did you learn about human nature from your study of the Bible?** Have each triad share their finding, first the left side, then the right side. Don't make comments as they are sharing. Instead move quickly from one group to the next, affirming their summaries.

5. DEBATE: When each group has shared, SAY: **There seems to be a difference of opinion here. One half of the room says that man is basically good, created in God's image; the other half is saying that mankind is basically sinful. These two ideas are opposites. Well, which is it? Which view is right?** Allow open discussion among the groups. Lead the discussion, not giving answers yet, but allowing the students to wrestle with the issue of how to bring together these two contradictory ideas. Play devil's advocate! If someone says both views are right, ask how two contradictory ideas can both be true since this is not logical reasoning?

6. SUMMARY: **This has been a good discussion. Actually, both sides are right. You see, the Bible indicates that human nature is BOTH good and bad. We are created in God's image, but we also inherit a sin nature from our human father, Adam.**

B. ILLUSTRATION: A "DOUBLE EXPOSURE": Bring out the camera as an object lesson. SAY: **Think of it this way. With a 35 mm camera you could take a picture; then without advancing the film, take another picture. This would expose the same frame of film twice. When you developed the film, both images would be printed, one superimposed on the other. This is called a "double exposure."**

1. GOD-IMAGE: **Human nature is like a double exposure. We are created in God's image; that's the first shot. This God-image is good. When we look around us we notice that even non-Christians can do good things. They give money to charitable causes and help little old ladies across the street. These are all good things which reflect the God-image within us.**

2. SIN NATURE: **But then, because of Adam's fall, we have a sinful nature superimposed onto God's image. That's the second shot.**

    a. "SIN" DEFINED: **But what exactly is "sin." Having a sin nature does not mean that we are as bad as we could be. It means that we are not as good as we ought to be, and that makes us look bad. In other words, we cannot live up to God's standards of perfection. Remember from our study of Theology what is God like?** (God is holy and righteous. He always does the right thing.) **But we are not holy and righteous. Romans 3:23 puts it this way: "For all have sinned and fall short of the glory of God."**

lesson 5

b. SAY: Some people today say that mankind is basically "good." But those who believe that have a hard time explaining why there is so much evil in the world. However, the Bible gives us the answer to the problem of evil. Because of our sin nature, we have the crime, anger, and hatred we see all around us. Only the biblical view of human nature can explain what we actually see and experience in the real world: the acts of kindness and the acts of evil.

C. TRANSITION: This view of human nature also has very specific implications for everyone's life. We will see how these implications are reflected in the other areas of a total worldview as we continue our study in the weeks ahead. But for today, we will zero in on one particular application that flows directly from the biblical view of psychology.

IV. APPLICATION

A. BROKEN RELATIONSHIP: Again, studying Theology, we learned that God is not only Righteous, but also Relational. The fact that we have a sin nature affects our relationship with God. Sin has severed that relationship. According to the passage in Genesis 3, when Adam and Eve sinned, God's punishment was to break off His relationship with them. This changed their entire basic nature. It superimposed a "sin nature" over their "image of God" nature.

1. SAY: Turn in your Bibles to Romans 5:12. Read it to the class and SAY: Here we learn that this sin nature was then passed on to Adam's children, and on down to us.

2. SAY: But God was not content to allow mankind to stay in this state of spiritual separation. Adam's sin set in motion a whole set of events leading up to the coming of God's Son, Jesus. Jesus dealt with our sin nature ultimately, by dying to take the punishment for our sin. In this way, two characteristics of God's nature were satisfied. His Righteousness was satisfied because the penalty for sin had been paid. God did this out of His love, thus allowing us to experience a Relationship with Him, which is the reason He created us.

B. JOHN 3:1-6: In John 3:1-6, Jesus gave a specific solution to mankind's basic sin problem. Let's all turn to John 3 and read verses 1- 6. Read the passage and then SAY:

1. SAY: In verse 3, Jesus talks about seeing the kingdom of God. This refers to having a relationship with God. ASK: In verse 3, what does Jesus say is the way to have a relationship with God? (We need to be born again.)

2. ASK: What does it mean to be "born again"? (It refers to a spiritual "birth," i.e. to be given a new nature in Christ.)

3. ASK: When does this "new birth" take place? (When a person acknowledges Jesus' payment on the cross for his sin nature and personally receives God's forgiveness.)

4. WRITE inside the person on the board the letters "N. N." for "New Nature." SAY: **At that point of new birth, a person is given a "new nature" in Christ.** Have everyone turn to **2 Corinthians 5:17** and read it out loud. **This says that if we are in Christ, we are a new creation. This means that the old sin nature has been defeated and a new nature, the Holy Spirit, comes to make you alive spiritually. When a person receives this new nature, he has a new desire to love God. He finds that reading the Bible is interesting, and he can understand it better. He wants to live according to God's standards. He is literally a new creature, from the inside out.**

5. SUMMARY: **So God has provided for us a way to be united with Him at the most basic level, a spiritual union. This provision is possible because Jesus Christ died for our sin problem, thus paving the way for God's love and forgiveness for our sins.**

C. APPLICATION: **But God's provision must be accepted by each individual. If you have not experienced a new birth by trusting Jesus with your sin problem, you can do it today.** At this point, you can handle the specific application in one of two ways. Carefully evaluate the students you are teaching. If you know that most are already Christians, #1 below will be the better choice.

1. OPTION A: Suggest that anyone who is not sure he is a Christian should talk privately with you after class. Then go to #3 below.

2. OPTION B: You can have a "pray-with-me" at this time. If you choose this option, then say a prayer out loud as a suggested prayer to receive Christ. It may be something like: "Lord Jesus, I need you. Thank you for dying on the cross for my sins. I accept your forgiveness for my sin nature. Thank you for forgiving me and giving me eternal life. Come into my life and make me the kind of person You want me to be." Have everyone bow in prayer and if anyone wants to accept Christ as his Savior, he can pray along silently as you repeat the prayer out loud, a phrase at a time.

3. ASSURANCE: Regardless of whether you do A or B above, continue by asking everyone to turn to **1 John 5:11-13** as you SAY: **The Bible tells us something about everyone who has entered into this relationship with God.**

   a. READ verse 11-12 out loud and SAY: **There are two kinds of people mentioned here. Who are they?** (those who have eternal life and those who do not) **So this passage is talking about two kinds of people, the "haves" and the "have nots."**

   b. READ verse 13 in this way: NOTE: IT'S IMPORTANT TO SAY THE FOLLOWING EXACTLY AS WRITTEN: **Now follow along as I read verse 13. "These things I have written to you who believe in the name of the Son of God, in order that you may," now this is a 'multiple-choice' question: think, hope or know, that you have eternal life." Which is it: think, hope or know?** (Know.) **Right!**

      (1) ASK: **Now if you know something and had to put it on a scale from zero to 100% sure, where would you put it?** (100%) **So this verse is saying that you can be 100% sure that you have eternal life if you believe what?** (You believe in the name of the Son of God.)

thinking like a christian

(2) SAY: **And according to John 1:12, believing in His name is equated with "receiving" Him and becoming God's child.**

V. CLOSING

    A. RECAP: **All of this is wrapped up in that idea of being born again: trusting in God's forgiveness through Jesus' payment on the cross, believing that Jesus died for your sins, receiving Christ's new nature into your life through the Holy Spirit, and becoming a child of God. WOW! We all should thank God often that Christ's Holy Spirit is in our life and that we have eternal life.**

    B. PLAY THE SONG, "GOD": If there is time, play the song by Rebecca St. James again. This time tell the group to listen carefully to the last stanza: "Lord I praise you for your endless love, Your boundless grace, I stand here amazed ... ." Mention that after recognizing God's creative power and filling the void in her soul through Jesus' sacrifice, the singer is left with praise on her lips for God's goodness and grace!

    C. PRAYER: This would be a good time to pause for group prayer. Suggest that anyone who wants to may thank God for being forgiven and for the new nature that accompanies that forgiveness.

    D. NEXT WEEK: **Some of you may be saying, "Yea, that's good about having a new nature in Jesus. But I still seem to sin. What's the problem?" We'll talk about that issue next week when we explore the next category on the worldview board: "Ethics." So be looking for examples during the week that fit into one of the categories of our worldview.**

    E. **STUDENT JOURNALS:** Remind students to spend time each day in their journal.

GOD

By Rebecca St. James & Tedd T.

Based on Psalm 8:4 - "What is man that You are mindful of him?"

He made the night
He made the day
Spread the earth upon the water
Made the heavens and the rain
Look at the sky see its design
The very same Creator is the one who gave us life
What is man that He's mindful of us?
We're merely clay in His hands
What am I that He loves me so much He would die
All that I can say is ...

CHORUS:
It's GOD truly GOD
Can you see can you hear can you touch can you feel
it's GOD truly GOD
I can't explain any other way cuz its GOD

Inside us all there is a void
All mankind is searching for the one who fills the soul
In Him there's hope in Him there's life
The world cries for a savior that's right before their eyes
What is man that He takes us in as His children to be His own
And what are we that He wants to be our Father
All that I can say is ...

CHORUS

Lord I praise You for Your endless love
Your boundless grace
I stand here amazed ...

CHORUS

Repeat

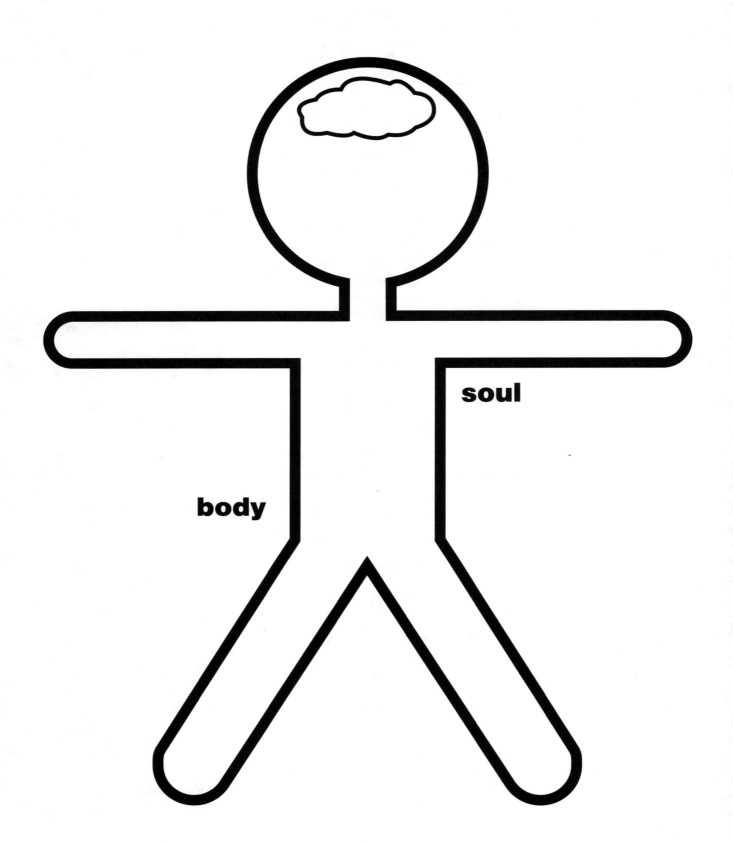

soul

body

lesson 6

ethics: what's right?

"Who's to say what's right and what's wrong? It all depends on the situation. What's right for you might not be right for me."

Comments like these have become the standard response by the majority of people today. With the loss of moral absolutes, our society is awash in a sea of ethical relativism. And the "relativistic bug" has bitten the majority of our youth and college students, even those that show up at your church every week.

This lack of a moral compass has left young people desperate to know what is right and what is wrong. Most make choices based on what is expedient for themselves. Others, even Christians, will make choices that they know are wrong because they believe they can "get away with it."

Because this issue of moral living has come under such attack over the past 30 years, we are witnessing more and more Christians who are failing to live by Godly standards. Christian youth are crumbling under the mounting pressure from the majority of their peers who live in opposition to biblical morality.

This lesson lays the groundwork upon which students can build a solid understanding of the biblical world-view of ethics. Ethics, consistent with what has already been studied under Theology, Philosophy, Biology, and Psychology, are part of a total worldview.

Not only will students see that they must rely on God's standards for right and wrong, but also they will learn to accept God's offer of forgiveness when they fail to make the right choice. This personal application will free them to return to walking in the light of God's moral truth, setting the stage for continued spiritual maturity.

As you prepare this lesson, pray for open hearts and minds of the students that you teach.

lesson six

ethics

key concept: Jesus Christ is the Light.

key verses: John 3: 19-20

"This is the verdict: Light has come into the world, but men loved darkness instead of light because their deeds were evil. Everyone who does evil hates the light, and will not come into the light for fear that his deeds will be exposed."

objectives: By the end of this lesson, each student should be able to

FOR THE REVIEW SESSION: PSYCHOLOGY

. . . state how humans are different from other animals.

. . . make the connection between psychology and the other worldview categories.

FOR NEW TOPIC: ETHICS

. . . explain how ethics are related to other worldview categories.

. . . discuss the relationship between ethics and the character of God.

. . . apply the principle of confessing their sins according to 1 John 1:9.

read: U.T.T., Chapter 14, Biblical Christian Ethics, p. 115.

before class:

FOR THE REVIEW SESSION: PSYCHOLOGY

☐ For each student make a copy of the handout, "**My Worldview of Psychology**" and have pencils available.

☐ Make an overhead cell or write on the board the Coles quote for Activity #4.

☐ Copy and cut apart the two "scenarios" on the "**Psychology Worldview Applied**" sheet and have available for the group discussion.

FOR THE NEW TOPIC: ETHICS

☐ Make a cassette tape using the script titled "Mission Possible." Have the tape and a tape player ready for class. NOTE: If you don't have equipment to make an audio tape, then enlist a student to read the script as you act it out.

☐ Have a yardstick or ruler as an object lesson during the introduction, but don't let students see it before you are ready to bring it out.

☐ During the week, find articles in the newspaper and magazines that deal with various ethical/moral issues such as abortion, euthanasia, homosexual behavior, homosexual marriage, pre-marital sex, etc. Cut them out and place them inside a large manila envelope.

☐ Have enough pencils and a sheet of lined 8 1/2 X 11 paper for each student for the Application at the end. You also will need a trash can in the classroom.

pre-class:

Before students come into class, be sure to draw a line on the board about 24 inches long.

lesson 6

thinking like a christian

PART ONE: REVIEW PSYCHOLOGY

1. THE WORLD OF IDEAS: As students come into class, continue to interact with them about their exploration of the "World of Ideas." Review any articles they bring in or some that you have brought, although don't disclose the articles you selected for the opening exercise on "Ethics." Have students share their articles with each other as they come into class.

2. SAY: **Last week we discussed "Psychology." Let's see how far we've come. Pretend there is a sophisticated computer robot in the room. What would you have to change about the robot for it to be human?** (This question is to get them thinking about what makes us "human" as opposed to being just a machine. Answers will vary, but should relate to our uniqueness in the mental/spiritual area.) Follow up questions:

   a. **If you could design your "hubot" (human + robot) any way you wanted, how would you design its moral capacity?** (This explores the issue of whether the hubot has a "free will," or is programmed to always choose the right things morally.)

   b. **If the hubot must always make the right choices morally, is he truly human?** (No, because he would not have "free will." The point is that free will is an indispensable human trait that God designed into humanity; without it there would be no opportunity to love freely and respond to God's love.)

   c. SUMMARIZE the discussion to include the importance of the human traits of moral free choice and a spiritual dimension as being unique among all of God's creation!

3. WORLDVIEW ANALYSIS: Go over to the bulletin board and point to the various pieces of the puzzle as you SAY: **Let's grasp a worldview for a moment.**

   a. **Christian psychology answers what question?** (What is the nature of mankind?)

   b. **What is the answer to that question from the Biblical Christian worldview?** (Human nature is a double exposure: God's image and sinful.)

   c. **How does our view of biology relate to psychology?** (We are created in God's image, not "evolved" from some primitive creature.)

   d. **How does philosophy relate to psychology?** (Man is a part of the real natural world, but also man has a spiritual dimension. We have a rational mind that can know the truth and relate to the spiritual realm.)

   e. **How does theology relate to psychology?** (There is a God who rules over the natural realm and who wants to relate in love to mankind according to His righteousness.)

   f. SUMMARY: **Do you see how all of these pieces are related to one another? They all fit together to form a whole picture of reality. The Bible relates to all of life!**

4. COLES QUOTE: Print the following quote on the board or on the overhead and HAVE STUDENTS COMMENT : "Nothing I have discovered about the make-up of human beings contradicts in any way what I learn from the Hebrew prophets such as Isaiah, Jeremiah and Amos, and from the book of Ecclesiastes, and from Jesus and the lives of those he touched. Anything I can say as a result of

lesson 6

my research into human behavior is a mere footnote to those lives in the Old and New Testaments."
- Robert Coles, Harvard psychiatrist, quoted in U.T.T. (Unabridged Version), p. 420.

You may stimulate responses with the following questions:
- **What connections does this Harvard psychiatrist make between modern psychology and the Bible?**
- **Do observations of human behavior support or contradict the biblical view?**
- **Can you think of any specific examples from your experience or from current events that support these conclusions?**

5. PARAGRAPH: Give each student a handout, "My Christian Worldview of Psychology," as you SAY: **Now, we will complete our paragraph on the Christian worldview of psychology. Let's fill in the blanks together.** The paragraph should read: "My Christian worldview of psychology states that man's basic nature is a <u>double</u> exposure. The first is a reflection of our being created in God's <u>image</u>. The second is our <u>sin</u> nature. The solution to the problem of sin and reestablishing a right relationship with God is a life given to <u>Jesus Christ</u>, who crucified my sin when He <u>died</u> on the cross for me, and rose again to give me <u>eternal</u> life."

6. APPLIED PSYCHOLOGY SCENARIOS: SAY: **Now let's put into practice some of the ideas we have been learning about a biblical worldview of psychology.** Divide the class into two groups, have them read their assigned scenario (found at the end of this lesson) and discuss the following questions in their group, then be prepared to share their insights with the other group. Allow 5 minutes for individual group discussions and another 5 minutes for each group report.

    DISCUSSION QUESTIONS:
    - What is the surface problem?
    - What is the root problem based on a Christian worldview?
    - What would you suggest as the solution to the problem?

7. SUMMARIZE THE REVIEW SESSION and MAKE THE TRANSITION into the new topic for this session by saying: **You can see that because of man's basic nature, there are going to be problems. Those problems are most keenly felt when we must make a choice between two conflicting ideas. Today's lesson is about making moral choices.**

PART TWO: NEW TOPIC - ETHICS

I. INTRODUCTION

    A. SAY: **I need to tell you about a strange thing that happened to me as I was coming into the building: a man wearing a hat and a trench coat handed me this tape and envelope. Maybe we better see what this is all about.** Have the taped script cued up and ready. Press the "Play" button on the recorder as you open the large envelope and begin pulling out the articles. Listen intently to the tape as you look over the articles. When the tape is over, turn off the player and SAY: **Well, it looks like we have quite a challenge before us today. How about it, gang, are you with me in this?** Drum up some enthusiasm with the class!

    B. LINE ILLUSTRATION: SAY: **The man on the tape said that our first task was to figure out the length of this line on the board. And if we can understand that, then we will be on our way to knowing how to make good moral**

thinking like a christian

choices in life. ASK SOMEONE: **How long is this line?** (Let him respond.) Turn to another and ASK: **How long do you think this line is?** (Let her respond.) Repeat the same question to one or two others without any comment.

1. SAY: **There seems to be a problem here. You've given me different answers to my question. Which answer is the right one? What do we need in order to know exactly how long the line is?** (A ruler, yardstick, etc.)

2. YARDSTICK: Bring out a ruler or yardstick and SAY: **Good idea! Here's a yardstick.** Take the yardstick and measure the line. Announce to the class the correct length. **But I don't understand how this helps us in the area of moral choices. Do you have any ideas?** (The yardstick is called an "objective standard." "Objective" means an object outside of you. It does not depend on your **subjective** feelings which are inside you. An objective standard acts as the final authority to settle any disputes about the length of this line. In the case of the yardstick, an inch is always an inch. It is an absolute. God's laws are also objective and unchanging...they are absolutes.)

3. SUMMARY: **So in order to know the right answer to something, we must have an absolute "standard," something that acts as a judge to settle disputes like we had about the length of the line. In the case of the line I drew, the yardstick with its constant "inch," was the "standard."**

C. CONTROVERSIES TODAY: **The same is true when it comes to settling disputes about morality. In our society today there are many controversies about what is right and what is wrong.** Read or briefly summarize some of the articles you collected. Do not discuss the issues at this point. Just bring out the fact that people have different ways of thinking about these moral issues.

1. SAY: **The question is: How do we settle these disputes? How do we know what to think about these issues? What is the right thing to do? When we ask these types of questions, we are moving into the area called "Ethics." "Ethics" answers the question: "What is right and wrong behavior?"**

2. TRANSITION: **So today, we will look at the category of "Ethics." First, let's visualize how ethics fits into the total picture of our biblical worldview.**

D. INTER-RELATIONAL DISCIPLINES: **Ethics is closely related to the other disciplines we have studied.**

1. THEOLOGY: **In our study of theology, we learned about God by studying His attributes, His character. As ruler, God is just. In relationships, He is fair; and in His righteousness, He exercises justice. All of these are ethical concepts.**

2. PHILOSOPHY: **What did we learn in Philosophy that expresses ethical truth?** (We learned that our minds can understand God's righteous character and also understand the difference between right and wrong. Also, we have the capacity to know what is right because God has given us an external, objective source for morals in the Bible.)

3. BIOLOGY: **What does biology have to do with ethics?** (God has designed the physical world to operate in certain ways, like the law of gravity. But also He designed our lives to be lived according to certain laws [e.g., the Ten Commandments]. This is built into the way we were created.)

thinking like a christian

4. PSYCHOLOGY: **How does psychology support biblical ethics?** (Human nature is designed and created in God's image. Because we are created in God's image, we know what is right to do; but because we have a sin nature, we do not always live up to the standards God has established.)

5. SUMMARY: **These four pieces of the worldview puzzle act as supports for another piece of the total picture. They form the foundation for understanding "ethics."**

E. TRANSITION: **Today, we will dig a little deeper into the biblical understanding of how we know what is right and, as Christians, what to do when we do the wrong thing.**

II. CHRISTIAN ETHICS COME FROM GOD

A. THREE LEVELS: **There are three ways that we come to know right from wrong. These three ways represent three different levels of understanding.** Draw three concentric circles with level 1 being the outermost circle.

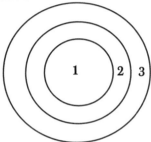

1. **ROMANS 2:14-15:** LEVEL 1 - LOOK IN YOURSELF: Have everyone turn to the passage and have someone read it out loud; then write the word "Conscience" with an arrow to the outermost circle.

   a. SAY: **These verses say that all people have a conscience. This is one way that God communicates to us His standards of right and wrong.**

      (1) ANGEL/DEVIL ILLUSTRATION: **There was a cartoon on T.V. a long time ago which showed a character trying to decide whether to do something that was not right. A little devil popped up on his left shoulder and said, "Do it!" Then an angel popped up on his right shoulder and said, "Don't do it!" Then the devil said, "Do it!" and the angel said, "Don't do it!" and back and forth, the cartoon character turning his head from side to side, listening to first one and then the other.**

      (2) ASK: **Have you ever felt that way before, like there was a struggle going on in your mind?** (various responses) **Do you want to tell us about a time you thought about doing something wrong but your conscience told you not to?** Allow several to share their experience.

      (3) ASK: **Why is our conscience not always a reliable guide in determining the right thing to do?** (Because it is subjective, or reflects how we feel.

There are times that we confuse the "angel" with the "devil." In other words, we listen to our feelings which lead us to do the wrong thing. They suppress our conscience which tells us to do what is right.)

b. DISCUSSION QUESTION: **Can you think of a way that your peers use their feelings to make decisions about what is right or wrong?** (When they feel "in love" and go too far sexually, or want to feel happy and use drugs, etc. Draw out the discussion as the class warms up to the question, asking for more examples. Move on to the next part of the outline before the discussion begins to drag.)

2. **DEUTERONOMY 29:29:** LEVEL 2 - LOOK IN THE SCRIPTURE. Have everyone look up the verse and someone read it out loud. Write the word "Scripture" beside the circles, with an arrow pointing to the second circle.

a. SAY: **The second level of knowing what is right is by looking in the Bible. God has revealed to us an objective standard in the moral laws found in the Bible.**

b. ASK: **What does the term "objective" mean?** (An objective standard exists outside of ourselves and is true for all people, in all places, at all times. It is absolute. It can be known. It is in contrast to "subjective," which means within ourselves and based on our feelings.) Relate God's objective standard to the line illustration at the beginning of the lesson.

c. SAY: **In the same way that the ruler was the objective standard to tell us the right length of the line, the Bible is God's objective standard that tells us the right way to live. It tells the truth, no matter how you feel. It's truth is unchanging. And the moral standards of the Bible are true for all people, in all situations, throughout all time.**

NOTE: Technically, the Bible does contain some "standards" that are specific to a certain time and people, such as some of the Old Testament laws that are directed to the nation of Israel before the advent of Christ. These laws do not apply to us today. It is not the purpose of this lesson to make that much of a distinction. However, if a student brings up the question, you should briefly answer it and move on.

3. **JOHN 1:14-18:** LEVEL 3 - LOOK AT JESUS: Have everyone turn to **John 1:14-18** and ask for a volunteer to read it. Then write the word "Jesus" in the innermost circle.

a. SAY: **Jesus Christ, as God, is the ultimate source for our standard of conduct. He is the "Truth" with a capital "T."**

b. ASK: **What is true about Jesus that would make Him the ultimate standard for what is right?** Refer back to the lesson on Theology and God's character: He is Ruler, Relational and Righteous.

(1) **God is Righteous; therefore, we are to do the "right" things. Because God is love, we are to love. Because God is gracious, we are to forgive. Because God is truth, we are to tell the truth. These characteristics flow from His nature. They reflect the way He is! He can be no other way.**

(2) **Why does God's truth not change?** (Because God's character does not change. That's why truth is the same for all people, in all places and at all times. God is the ultimate standard for ethics.)

4. APPLY IT!: **Think about it for a minute. God's standards are true for all people, in all places, at all times, right? Let's check it out to see if that idea fits into the real world. Take a certain type of behavior and elevate it to an absolute standard.**

   a. LOVE: **For example, take love. What if everyone everywhere expressed love to other people? What would be the result?** (The world would be a great place to live!) Have students describe the details of what it would be like for everyone to behave in a loving way. What would be the results for individuals...for families...for society?

   b. HATE: **O.K., now let's take another type of behavior, hate. What if everyone everywhere expressed hate to other people? What would be the result?** (War, violence, rape, murder, etc.) Draw this out for more details. How would it affect their personal lives? Have students suggest other examples that they might think of. Continue this as time allows, but be sure to save enough time to cover part III, "How to Handle Failure."

   c. SAY: **You can see that God's standards are true for all people, and they are the standards that make the world the best possible place.**

B. SUMMARY: **That's why God has given us ethical standards to live by. The world works better for us if we cooperate with those standards. Ethics are not meant to make us feel tied down, or make life boring and dull, but to protect us and provide for us out of God's love.**

C. TRANSITION: **Yet there are times that we fail to live according to God's standards. So what do we do when that happens?**

III. HOW TO HANDLE FAILURE

A. REVIEW: **You recall from last week, from our study of Psychology, that you have a new nature in Christ. Even though Christ has given you a new nature, sometimes we decide to live by our own standards instead of God's. Since we are not hubots (part human and part robot), we have the choice to obey or disobey God's moral code.**

B. WHO'S DRIVING? **Think of your Christian life as a car.** Draw the following ideas on the board using a front seat and back seat profile of a car. Put "H. S." (for Holy Spirit) in the front seat and "Flesh" in the back seat as you SAY:

   1. EXPLAIN: **God's Spirit is in the driver's seat, directing your life according to His will. This new nature, the Holy Spirit, is living in you and guiding you. But your flesh is still in the car, too, sitting in the back seat.**

thinking like a christian

a. SAY: **The "flesh" does not refer to your "skin," but to your entire body and soul which developed the habit of disobeying God. In other words, before you became a Christian, your "old sinful nature" directed your body into sinful patterns of behavior. These sinful patterns became habits in your mind and expressed themselves through your body.**

b. EXAMPLE: **For example, before becoming Christians, you guys could look at a gorgeous girl in a skimpy two-piece bathing suit, and the old nature would begin to transmit lustful thoughts and ideas to your brain, and your body would respond to those ideas. According to Romans 6:6-12, once you became a Christian, your old nature died and you were given a new nature from Christ, and your bodies became a temple of the Holy Spirit. However, when you now look at a gorgeous girl in a skimpy two-piece bathing suit, your old nature has some competition and your lust of the flesh will be subdued by the degree to which you are under the control of the new nature and the Holy Spirit.**

2. DRAW another car profile but this time put "Flesh" in the front and "H. S." in the back as you SAY: **There are times that you succumb to the desires of the flesh and decide that YOU want to do things YOUR way instead of God's way. So you jump over the seat and take over the driving. This is what happens when you sin. It may be a fit of anger at your brother or sister, it may be lying to your parents, it may be choosing to be sexually active. These sinful thoughts and acts have pushed the Holy Spirit out of the driver's seat and placed you right smack dab behind the wheel. This breaks off your communication with God. When that happens, you need to know what to do about it.**

3. APPLICATION: HOW TO BE FILLED WITH THE HOLY SPIRIT: **Here's how to put the Holy Spirit back in the driver's seat by remembering the "ABC's" of confession.**

a. AGREE: **The "A" stands for "Agree" with God that what you did was wrong. Confess the sin to God according to 1 John 1:9.** Have everyone find 1 John 1:9 in their Bibles as you read it out loud. Then SAY: **Confess means to "agree with" God what you did was wrong according to His standards of rightness and you don't want to do it again.**

b. BELIEVE: **Next is the "B," which stands for "Believe" God's promise in 1 John 1:9 to cleanse you of all unrighteousness.** Relate God's righteousness back to our study of theology where we learned that God is Ruler, Relational and Righteous.

c. CONTROL: **Then comes the "C" for "Control." You should give "Control" of your life back to Him by asking Christ to again take over the driver's seat in your life. This means allowing Jesus to set the standard for your decisions and behavior.**

C. SIN LIST: **Let's practice what we've discussed today. You will spend a few minutes in individual, silent prayer. Ask God to point out any areas in your life that are displeasing to Him.**

thinking like a christian

1. SAY: **On the piece of paper I'm handing out, write out any specific sins that come to your mind. This is just for you to do by yourself.** Allow a few minutes to complete their list. As they are writing, you write on the board 1 John 1:9, the entire verse.

2. SAY: **When you have completed your list, write over the sheet in big letters the entire verse from 1 John 1:9, and thank God that you are forgiven and cleansed.**

3. AFTER they are done, have them tear up their lists and throw the pieces in the trash. SAY: **God says that He forgives you and cleanses you. He says that He remembers your sins no more, so we can forget about them, too. Practicing the "ABC's" of confession should be repeated any time you realize that you have sinned. In this way, you will be walking in the light of God's love and will experience closer fellowship with Him day by day.**

IV. SUMMARY:

A. MISSION POSSIBLE: **It seems like an impossible mission - to live the Christian life and walk in the light of God's Word. But God has made it a possible mission by creating a way for us to restore our fellowship with Him when we sin. And He has given us the Holy Spirit to nudge us when we sin and encourage us to ask for forgiveness. To help you make the right choices each day, be sure and spend time each day in your Student Journal. The exercises will help you solidify what you are learning in our group session. Remember, when we fail, God has provided a way to experience His forgiveness in the "ABC's" of confession.**

B. CLOSE IN PRAYER.

C. REMIND STUDENTS to continue to study in their **student journal** each day, and to be on the lookout for articles that relate to ethics or any of the other categories already studied.

psychology worldview applied

SCENARIO #1:

Bobbie is from a broken home in a rundown neighborhood. She is often embarrassed at school because her clothes are from Wal-mart and the Salvation Army. While at the mall one day, she decides to try on a great-looking outfit. But since she does not have the money to buy it, she puts on her own clothes over the new outfit and starts to leave the store. She is caught and arrested. She is released to her parent and sent to a first-offender counseling program.

DISCUSSION QUESTIONS:
- What is the surface problem?

- What is the root problem based on a Christian worldview?

- What would you suggest as the solution to the problem?

SCENARIO #2:

George and Mary have been dating for six months. They are really in love and believe that they are "right" for each other. George is pressuring Mary toward sexual involvement. Mary knows that many of her friends are sexually active and she feels bad for not meeting Robert's "need" in this way. She finally gives in to sexual involvement, believing that one day they will be married anyway; besides, it really feels nice being loved. However, afterwards she experiences intense feelings of guilt. She becomes uncomfortable going to church and being around her Christian friends. George says that her personality has changed and that she is not as much fun to be around anymore. He considers breaking off their relationship.

DISCUSSION QUESTIONS:
- What is the surface problem?

- What is the root problem based on a Christian worldview?

- What would you suggest as the solution to the problem?

My Christian

Worldview

of Psychology

My Christian worldview of psychology states that man's basic nature is a _____exposure. The

first is a reflection of our being created in God's _____. The second is our _____nature.

The solution to the problem of sin and reestablishing a right relationship with God is a life given to

_____ _____, who crucified my sin when he _____on the cross for me, and

rose again to give me _____life.

mission possible script

Record the following on a cassette tape. Read it in a deep voice.

Good morning, (your name: Mr./Mrs./Ms._____). As you are aware, there is a growing problem in America. People everywhere, especially students, are trapped in a maze of conflicting ideas concerning how they should live. This moral maze is filled with a variety of major life-style choices concerning issues such as abortion, euthanasia, homosexual behavior, homosexual marriage, and pre-marital sex. Plus, there are the day-to-day choices of whether to cheat on a test or tell the truth to parents. These and other ethical choices seem harder and harder to make because of the cultural smog that has settled over this maze of choices.

Your mission, Mr./Mrs./Ms. _____, should you choose to accept it, is to help the students in your class to break through the cultural smog and navigate a clear course through the moral maze. Contrary to other missions, this one is possible. The first task for your Mission Possible team is to determine the length of the line drawn on the board in your room. If they can figure out the principle behind how to tell the length of that line, then they will be well on their way to understanding how to make good moral choices.

Good luck, Mr./Mrs./Ms. _____. I have full confidence in your ability to fulfill this mission. Your Mission Possible team are no dummies. They will help you accomplish this mission.

Oh, and Mr./Mrs./Ms. _____, this tape will NOT self-destruct in 5 seconds. We can't afford to keep buying new tapes!

notes & ideas

thinking like a christian

lesson 7

sociology: what about relationships?

Unless you are planning to live as a hermit in the Himalayas, you will be living around other people; and anytime there is more than one person in the room, there is potential for conflict. The question which naturally arises, "How should we live together in groups?", brings us to this week's lesson on Sociology.

The Bible makes it clear that relationships are basic to the human experience. You will recall that the first relationship was among the three persons of the Godhead; God the Father, Son, and Holy Spirit. There was love and communication before the foundation of the earth was laid. As image-bearers of God, we are endowed with the same abilities and desires for personal interaction.

Yet, because of our sin nature, relationships come with much difficulty. God has established various levels of "group living" to meet our need for community. The **family** serves as the foundational level to impart new life, nurture children spiritually/morally/emotionally toward maturity, and care for our physical needs. The **church** functions as the second line of defense for meeting the spiritual, emotional and physical needs of people outside the immediate family. Finally, the **state** is designed to secure a safe overall community in which individuals can express their God-given talents.

In our culture today there is much confusion over social issues. Arriving at a definition of "family," determining the role of the church in society, assessing the proper scope of government, young people are expected to wade through an incredible mix of ideas. That is why this study is extremely important. It could mean the difference between a cultural meltdown or a renaissance of Christian values, ideas and beliefs.

From a biblical standpoint, this study of sociology brings many disciplines into focus. It is easy to see the worldview connections as all the categories studied so far form the framework for this topic. Biblical Theology, Philosophy, Biology, Psychology and Ethics all blend together in exploring this area of social living. This consistency marks the beauty of a worldview approach to learning. As you begin to sense this awesome cohesion, be sure to share those thoughts with the students you are teaching. What you teach is often "caught" from your enthusiasm as much as it is "taught" by your words.

Pray for God the Holy Spirit's infilling as you prepare for this week's lesson and that lights will be popping on in the minds of those you teach, as they realize the incredible unity and practicality of a consistent biblical worldview!

sociology

key concept: Jesus Christ is the Son.

key verse: Isaiah 9:6
"For unto us a child is born, unto us a son is given, and the government shall be upon his shoulders, and his name shall be called Wonderful Counselor, Mighty God, Everlasting Father, Prince of Peace."

objectives: By the end of this lesson, each student should be able to

FOR THE REVIEW SESSION: ETHICS
. . . anticipate the consequences of making wrong moral choices.
. . . defend a biblical ethic related to current issues such as abortion.

FOR NEW TOPIC: SOCIOLOGY
. . . understand three biblical institutions established by God: the family, the church, and the state.
. . . apply biblical principles to a current social problem.

read: U.T.T., Chapter 26, Biblical Christian Sociology.

before class:

☐ Make copies of the following handouts for your students: **"Task Force on Social Problems," "Living in Society: A Biblical View,"** and **"My Christian Worldview of Ethics."**

☐ Have a pencil or pen for every student.

☐ Look through newspapers or magazines to find articles dealing with current social issues such as teen pregnancy, drug abuse, child abuse, alcoholism, crime, divorce, or homosexuality. Bring these to class to be used during the "Task Force" phase of the lesson. NOTE: These issues can also be considered "ethical" issues; yet because they deal with people's interaction with others, they fit under "social" themes as well.

☐ Bring a pair of sunglasses to wear for the "Task Force" exercise.

PART ONE: REVIEW ETHICS

1. THE WORLD OF IDEAS: As they come into class, interact with students about the current issues in the news and the worldview implications. (Save any social issues until the end of class.)

2. DISCUSS: Read the following verses, one at a time, or have them written on the board. Ask the discussion questions that follow:

   a. **Proverbs 14:12: "There is a way that seems right to a man, but in the end it leads to death."**
      1) ASK: **How does this verse relate to our study of ethics?**

      2) ASK: **In what ways could following man's ways lead to death?**

   b. **Proverbs 14:15: "The simple believes everything, but the prudent man considers his steps."**
      1) ASK: **Where do you get information about life? List several sources:**

      2) ASK: **Should you "believe everything you hear"?**

      3) ASK: **What does it mean to "consider [your] steps"?**

      4) ASK: **How can you be "prudent" (wise) in deciding which step to take?**

3. DISCUSS the chart from the **STUDENT JOURNAL,** Week 6, Day 2, concerning GOD'S MORAL PLAN and CONSEQUENCES of following and not following God's plan based on the following verses: Genesis 2:22-24; Proverbs 12:22; Matthew 6:25-27; 1 Corinthians 6:18-20. Have different students read a passage and discuss the headings. Help students think specifically about each issue and relate it to situations that they may know about personally. Don't be satisfied with vague or general answers. Summarize their comments as you SAY: **You will recall that earlier in this series we learned that "IDEAS HAVE CONSEQUENCES." If we follow man's distorted ideas about God's moral design, there are significant and negative consequences to those actions.**

4. DISCUSS current ethical issues that you have found in the news from the past several weeks; such as abortion, homosexuality, cloning, kids killing kids, etc. Lead students to discover how to approach each issue from a biblical worldview by thinking about how each issue relates to the major categories (i.e., Theology, Philosophy, Biology, etc.)

   EXAMPLE: "Abortion" - SAY: **In the current debate over abortion, the question is couched as a "rights" issue, i.e., the "right" of the woman to control her own body and when "life" begins. ASK: According to the Bible, what "rights" do we have before God?** (See I Cor. 6:19-20; Phil. 2:3-5) **What is the biblical view of "life"?** (See Psalm 139:13-16; Genesis 1:27). **Think through each worldview category. What would a biblical worldview tell us about how that category relates to the issue of abortion?** The following are suggestions to stimulate their thinking:

   • **Theology:** God desires a relationship with mankind; therefore, each child is special to God. God is righteous. Thus we should find out what His perspective is on abortion and not just do what might be convenient to us. God is Ruler over the universe, which means that He can enforce His righteous judgment on people who disobey Him.

- **Philosophy:** Mankind has a spiritual dimension as well as a physical body. Therefore, a woman should consider the spiritual consequences of aborting a child, not just the immediate physical aspects.
- **Biology:** God created mankind. Therefore unborn children are not just "blobs of protoplasm," but special people in God's sight.
- **Psychology:** We are created in God's image, a special and unique position among all of His creatures. Yet our sin nature leads us to do wrong things, such as killing the unborn.
- **Ethics:** God has established certain rules of conduct, such as "Do not murder." These standards are absolute and true for all people including high school students. Therefore, abortion is not just a personal decision based on personal convenience. Aborting an unborn child is murdering an innocent victim. Teenagers slaughtering their classmates is also murdering innocent victims.

5. PARAGRAPH ON ETHICS: **It's time for us to construct our paragraph titled, "My Christian Worldview of Ethics." Please take that handout and fill in the blank spaces as we work through it together:** The paragraph should read: My Christian worldview of ethics states that God has provided an absolute ethical **standard** for me. I do not need to wonder what is **right** and what is **wrong**. He reveals this standard through my **conscience**, through His **Holy Scriptures**, and through **Jesus Christ**. God's truth does not **change**. When I fail to meet God's **standards**, I can use the **ABC** process to experience God's forgiveness. "A" stands for **Agree** (I must agree that I have **failed.**), "B" stands for **Believe** (I must believe that Christ offers me forgiveness through his work on the Cross.) and "C" stands for **Control** (I must allow the Holy Spirit to control my life in Christ.). This mission is **possible**, because Christ restores my **fellowship** with God.

PART TWO: NEW TOPIC: SOCIOLOGY

I. INTRODUCTION

A. PRESIDENTIAL TASK FORCE: Put on the SUNGLASSES as you SAY IN AN OFFICIAL, DEEP VOICE: **Good morning men and women. The reason I've called you here today is that your country needs you. The President of the United States has asked you to be on a special "Task Force" for solving social problems. But before you can implement concrete solutions, you must first identify the root causes.** Give every student a handout, "Task Force on Social Problems" as you SAY: **In a moment you will be divided into groups of 3 or 4. In your groups you will choose one of the following social problems on this piece of paper and decide what is the root cause of that particular problem. As you brainstorm together on the root cause, everyone write down your answer. Then, the person whose birthday is closest to June 1st will report your findings to the rest of us. Do your work well. Remember, the President and all of America are counting on you! You have four minutes to complete your task. Gather into teams of three at this time and begin your group session. Do not try to answer the "Solution" question yet. That comes later.**

1. CIRCULATE to each group and as they decide on one of the issues, hand them an article from the newspaper that relates to that issue. This brings the discussion down to real life examples instead of just vague generalities. The group can use the article in their discussion to put a "face" on the issue.

thinking like a christian

2. SHARING: After 4 minutes, have each Triad share what they wrote. You may lead a short discussion based on their comments, but do not get into long commentaries at this point.

    a. ASK LEADING QUESTIONS to help them see that root causes are always related to one of the four foundational categories of Theology, Philosophy, Biology, and Psychology.

    b. FOR EXAMPLE: As a group comes to the issue of using illegal drugs, you might share with the class this quote from Dr. Louis Sullivan, Secretary of Health and Human Services. He told the Parents Resource Institute for Drug Education in Nashville on March 15, 1991: "One of the key factors influencing attitudes about drug use--the perception of risk, and the approval or disapproval of drug use--is religious influence." This is based on a 1990 study of over 70,000 high school seniors. The point: the main reason that teens stay away from illegal drugs is because of their religious beliefs, i.e. their Theology, what they believe about God! Therefore, the real root cause of drug abuse is Theological, or religious in nature.

    c. SUMMARY: Summarize their comments. Resist talking about the solutions at this time. Save that for the Application at the end of the lesson.

    d. SAY: **Thank you for your participation in this "Task Force." The President thanks you, too. We may call on you at a later time for more of your wisdom and insight.** Take off the SUNGLASSES as you resume your "normal" voice.

3. ASK: **Why do we call these "social" problems? Aren't they just individual problems?** (They are social problems because they affect other people as well. An individual may take drugs by himself, but his drug habit always results in behavior that affects other people; he may steal to pay for his addiction, or he may get violent and abuse other people in his family, or he may influence others to take illegal drugs, etc.)

B. TRANSITION: **These social problems cause us to ask a question: "How can we build a healthy society"? So today we are going to look into the Bible to see if it helps us answer that question. Which of the 10 categories relates to this question concerning building a healthy society?** (Sociology) **Sociology is the study of social relationships. It answers the question, "How should we live together in groups"?** (Write that sentence on the board) **So first let's get some perspective on how sociology fits into our worldview picture.**

II. BIBLICAL SOCIOLOGY

A. SOCIOLOGY'S RELATIONSHIP TO OTHER DISCIPLINES: Review the four disciplines as they relate to sociology:

1. SAY: **Like Ethics, Sociology is related to these four foundational areas.**

    a. THEOLOGY: ASK: **Think with me a minute, how does Theology, our understanding of God, relate to Sociology?** (God created the human as a social being, with the need to relate to other beings. This was not done as an accident.)

    (1) SAY: **Back in Genesis 1 & 2, God said something about Adam soon after he was created. Do you know what God said?** ("It is not good for man to be alone. I will make him a helper suitable for him." - Genesis 2:18...I LOVE THAT

VERSE!) **This means that God intended for us to live with other people and not be loners.**

(2) ASK: **But guess what else? The idea of relationships started even before God created Adam and Eve. Relationships were around before people. Do you know how?** (The Trinity of God the Father, God the Son and God the Holy Spirit were in fellowship before the world was created, from eternity past!) **So relationships come from the very nature of God. They have always existed. And God extended that idea into His creation when He created Adam and Eve. And I'm glad He did!**

b. PHILOSOPHY: ASK: **Let's look at the next discipline. How does Philosophy relate to Sociology?** (Because God has told us about himself and ourselves through the Bible, we can know what is true about human relationships and how we should live together in society. Social relationships do not originate just from a certain cultural tradition, but from the inspired Word of God. We can know for certain how our society should be structured.)

c. BIOLOGY: ASK: **How does our Christian view of Biology help us understand Sociology?** (Because we are created distinct from the animals, we have a unique relationship with one another that is different from what animals experience. Unlike the animals we have a spiritual dimension to our lives.)

(1) DISCUSS: **Some sociologists study gorillas and how they live together in groups and then relate these observations to the human species. They say that they can learn about how we should live based on how gorilla's live together. Why do some people choose to study nature in order to understand people better?** (They believe that humans are just a part of nature, another "species" of animal, and share traits with other species in the animal kingdom.)

(2) ASK: **Does the study of other animals have limits as to its effectiveness?** (Yes.) **Why?** (Other species do not have a spiritual dimension.)

(3) SPIDER ILLUSTRATION: **The female black widow spider kills her mate after he has fertilized her eggs! Should women follow the spider's actions?** (Do I need to say it? NOOOO!)

d. PSYCHOLOGY: ASK: **Finally, how is Psychology foundational to Sociology?** (Our sin nature causes us to be alienated not only from God, but also from one another. Sin shows it's ugly head in the form of envy, hate, harsh words, talking behind someone's back, lying, stealing, etc., etc. Yet, because we are created in God's image, we all desire to be treated with fairness and love. So when we are not treated in that way, we do not experience the close relationships that we long to have. In the context of the family, church and the state, we learn to control our sinful tendencies by God's grace and power.)

2. TRANSITION: **So then, with this foundation, what can we learn about how we should relate to each other? Let's see what the Bible tells us about how to live a happier life together with other people. For this next section, we will take a short fantasy voyage.**

thinking like a christian

B. **DESERTED ISLAND EXERCISE:** **You have been shipwrecked with the others in your class on a deserted island in the South Pacific. It has become apparent after 30 days that you will not be rescued. You will have to organize yourselves as best you can to live together. But because you were all adrift for four days in small rafts before you landed on this island, the sun fried your brains and you all have mild cases of amnesia. As a result, you cannot remember how you used to live together. The only thing salvaged from the ship was a Bible. So you start searching the Bible to try to discover the best way to organize yourselves into your new society. Let's get into three groups. Each group will do some research into one of the social relationships listed on your handout and then report to the rest of us what they found.** Divide the class into three DISCOVERY GROUPS. Give to each student a copy of the handout, "Living in Society: A Biblical View." **You'll have seven minutes to study your particular relationship and record your answers on the handout. Then be prepared to have one person report to the entire class.** Give a one minute warning after 6 minutes. Have each group give their report. Suggested answers are given below:

1. THE FAMILY:

   a. Genesis 2:22-24 - Why would the family be a basic building block of society? (That is how the human race continues and how children learn about life.)

   b. Genesis 24:5 & Eph. 5:24-25 - How does God view the importance of establishing a meaningful relationship between husband and wife? (a one-year honeymoon and emphasis on loving and serving one another)

   c. Deuteronomy 6:4-9; 20-21; Joshua 4:4-7; Ephessians 6:4 - What role do parents play in the lives of their children? (instructing them in lessons of history to relate to God's work in the world; passing on these truths to children)

2. THE CHURCH:

   a. Romans 12:4-5; 1 Corinthians 12:12-14, 27; Colossians 1:18 - What illustration is given to represent the church? How does the church function like a "body"? Who is the "head"? (a "body"; it has different parts yet works together as in unison; Jesus)

   b. Why is the church important to the preservation of society? (The church is the means for moral and spiritual instruction, without which society would fall apart.)

3. THE STATE:

   a. Genesis 9:6 - How does this verse lay the foundation for civil government? (The government is God's means to bring about justice on earth by punishing a wrong-doer.)

   b. Romans 13:1-4 - What are the two major purposes given for the role of government? (to protect those who are good and punish those who do evil)

   c. 1 Timothy 2:1-4 - Why should we pray for those in authority over us? (so we may lead a quiet life of godliness and dignity)

4. **SUMMARY:** These three institutions--the family, the church, and the state-- together define the biblical worldview for living together in society. They provide a unique way to insure that individuals are cared for and nurtured. And they encompass a complete set of living conditions upon which society as a whole can grow and prosper in peace and freedom.

5. **TRANSITION: Each sphere has it's own area of influence. But there is a potential for conflict between these three institutions. Can you think of ways that there might be conflict?** (The state might try to take over the responsibilities of the family or church; or the church might try to take over responsibilities of the state, etc.) **Therefore, we need to see how these three areas can work together.**

III. BUILDING A SOCIETY

A. **SAY: Again, here you are on your deserted island. If you were to build your society based on these three biblical institutions we just discussed, how would you rank them in order of importance? Let's build a "society house."**

1. **ASK: Which one should we put first as the foundation? Defend your choice with reasons.** (The family is the foundation because it is the smallest social unit. No other person in society, such as those in the church or government, have the same depth of love and care for you as those in your own family. Therefore, the family is best able to pass on the values and spiritual vitality to the next generation. This is the biblical view according to Deu. 6, where parents are to instruct their own children.) While this is being discussed, draw out their reasons as you DRAW a three story house in which to write "Family," "Church," and "Government"- one on each level. Other questions might be: **Why is the family better able to transmit values than the church or government? What if there is a dysfunctional family? Maybe the government is better able to raise children?** (A dysfunctional family is not normal; it is the exception to the role of most good families. You don't make a rule for society based on the exceptional case. The role of government is to maintain order in society, not raise children.)

2. **ASK: Which would you place next, on the second level? Why?** (The church, because it is the next larger level of society within which we live and build relationships. Jesus said that nothing can prevail against His church - [see Matthew 16:18]. Also, God is more concerned about mankind's spiritual development than any other area, such as civil policy of the state.)

3. **ASK: Why should we place government on the third level?** (Because the state does have a legitimate place in securing peace and safety so that God's spiritual purposes can be carried out through the church and the family. But good government is based on good families and good churches doing their jobs first.)

B. **DISCUSS: What does each institution have in common with the other two as it relates to the individual? In other words, since you are a member of a family, a church, and a government, how do you relate to each one?** (I submit to my parents, church leaders, and government rulers)

1. BIBLICAL RANKING: **Remember that all three are important, but the Bible gives us a ranking of importance. Who will read Acts 4:18-20, and someone else, Acts 5:29-32?** (Peter and John arrested and brought before the religious rulers.)

2. DISCUSS: **What principle in these verses is related to obeying those in authority over us?** (We must obey God rather than man. This means that the state should not interfere with the godly purposes of the family and the church.) You may want to read to the class or put on the overhead the following quote from U.T.T., p. 481: "The state cannot give meaning or function; it must itself derive meaning and direction from the free society under God, one able to realize itself in terms of its image mandate."

3. SUMMARIZE the discussion so far from the deserted island exercise. **Therefore, we understand that the family, the church, and the state owe their existence to the will of God. He created these means of ordering society for His purposes, and each institution is accountable to Him and His moral will. When there is a conflict among them, your first allegiance is to God, then the family, after that the church, and finally the state.**

C. TRANSITION: **Now it's time to come back from our deserted island to the real world of the here and now and see how these ideas fit into real life situations. The Bible's view of sociology is not some abstract concept floating around in space out there, but it offers real, practical ways to improve how you live each day. Do you want to be happy in your relationships with other people? The biblical worldview offers concrete solutions to today's problems. Let's look at some of these problems and ways to improve the living conditions of ourselves and the people around us.**

IV. APPLIED BIBLICAL SOCIOLOGY

A. RECONVENE TASK FORCE: Put the SUNGLASSES back on as you SAY IN AN OFFICIAL DEEP VOICE: **We will now reconvene the President's Task Force on Social Problems. The President wants you to take the problem that you addressed earlier, and based on the root cause, come up with a solution to the problem. You need to get back into your original groups of three and address the same problem for which you discovered the root cause. Answer that second question on the handout. You have five minutes to work on a solution. Make it as specific as possible.**

1. REPORTS: Call the groups together for their reports. Encourage them to think more specifically if they tend to be too general. For example, don't settle for solutions like: "Teach kids not to take drugs." The solution does not fit the cause. That is an educational solution, but as we noted earlier the root cause is theological, or religious. If the root cause was ignorance, then an educational solution would be called for. But if the root cause is theological, then a religious solution is needed.

2. EXAMPLE: Problem: illegal drug use. Root cause: lack of a positive self-concept due to an improper worldview of God. The cause is religious in nature. Solution: Help more teens to understand the real significance of the love, forgiveness, and meaning to life that Jesus Christ offers to them; then they will not be drawn to the artificial "high" of taking drugs.

3. GOOD QUOTE!: You might want to copy the following quote onto an overhead cell or read it to the group after they deal with the issue of illegal drug use. David Zwiebel, member of the National Commission on Children, testified before the Senate Labor and Human Resources Committee:

"...it is clear to me that children who are nurtured with the foundations of faith and community that religious institutions provide are far better able to withstand the pressures and dangers they face in their everyday lives. Indeed statistics bear this out: Children who attend religious schools and are exposed to a rigorous program of moral training are far less likely to fall prey to the temptations of drugs, far less likely to drop out of school, far less likely to contribute to the epidemic of teen pregnancy, far less likely to engage in activities that are dangerous to themselves and dangerous to society. . . .I submit that our nation's interests would be well served by encouraging the active involvement of religious entities in the lives of impressionable children to the full extent permissible under the First Amendment." (Quoted in "Free to Be Family," a special report from the Family Research Council, p. 6-13.)

   a. ASK: **Why are teens less likely to be involved in these immoral activities if they attend church?** (Review ideas from last week's "Ethics" lesson and **Student Journal** assignments.)

   b. ASK: **What is his solution?** (To encourage active involvement in religious entities.) **What are "religious entities"?** (The church, or synagogue, and also the family!)

B. SUMMARY OF REPORTS: Summarize the reports and thank each team for their input. Then SAY: **We see from this study that a biblical worldview has specific application for our society today. The principles found in the Bible relate to current situations in life. But doesn't that just make sense? Human behavior and relationships are basically the same, no matter who the people are or where they live, or even when they lived. This commonality of human experience means that God's principles work all the time, in every place, with all people. As Christians, we hold the answers to the problems of the world! It's our task to get that message out to others.**

C. PRAYER: In groups of three, pray for the boldness to share biblical solutions with friends and classmates, face to face or in the form of papers written for class assignments. Encourage them to think "biblically" in every area of their lives and live it out!

D. THIS WEEK: Encourage students to do the "On the home front..." ideas on their handout and continue to spend time each day in their **Student Journal.**

thinking like a christian

living in society:

the family:

GENESIS 2:22-24 - Why would the family be a basic building block of society?

GENESIS 24:5 & EPHESIANS 5:24-25 - How does God view the importance of establishing a meaningful relationship between husband and wife?

DEUTERONOMY 6:4-9; 20-21; JOSHUA 4:4-7; EPHESIANS 6:4 - What role do parents play in the lives of their children?

the church:

ROMANS 12:4-5; 1 CORINTHIANS 12:12-14, 27; COLOSSIANS 1:18 - What illustration is given to represent the church? How does the church function like a "body"? Who is the "head"?

Why is the church important to the preservation of society?

the state:

GENESIS 9:6 - How does this verse lay the foundation for civil government?

ROMANS 13:1-4 - What are the two primary purposes given for the role of government?

1 TIMOTHY 2:1-4 - Why should we pray for those in authority over us?

task force on
social problems

Pick one of the following social problems and circle it. Then, answer question number 1:

Current social problems: teen pregnancy, teens killing teens, drug abuse, child abuse, alcoholism, STD's (Sexually Transmitted Diseases), crime, abortion, divorce, homosexuality.

1. WHAT IS THE ROOT CAUSE OF THE PROBLEM YOU CIRCLED? (Be specific.)

(DO NOT ANSWER QUESTION #2 UNTIL INSTRUCTED TO DO SO)

2. BASED ON A BIBLICAL WORLDVIEW, WHAT ARE SOME POSSIBLE SOLUTIONS TO THE ABOVE PROBLEM?

on the home front . . .

1) Ask your parents or grandparents what it was like growing up in their family and what society was like.

2) As a family, look for examples that "normalize" sinful behavior as presented in the newspapers, on T.V., through music, in the movies, etc. and discuss its impact on our society.

3) Together, make a list of the things you can do to strengthen your family relationships. (Be specific.)

thinking like a christian

My Christian

Worldview

of Ethics

My Christian worldview of ethics states that God has provided an absolute ethical _____ for me. I do

not need to wonder what is _____ and what is _____. He reveals this standard through my

_____, through His _____ _____, and through _____

_____. God's truth does not _____. When I fail to meet God's _____, I

can use the _____ process to experience God's forgiveness. "A" stands for _____(I must agree

that I have _____.), "B" stands for _____(I must believe that Christ offers me forgiveness

through His work on the cross.), and "C" stands for _____(I must allow the Holy Spirit to

control my life in Christ.). This mission is _____,because Christ restores my

_____with God.

notes & ideas

lesson 8

law: what are the rules?

Most students view "laws" as things to be avoided. They figure that anytime there is a rule, the idea is to see how far you can go and still get away with it. Since they have this negative understanding of the subject, your task this week will be to show them the positive benefits of laws.

This begins by understanding that everything about our world is based on "law." Laws are simply descriptions of what is true about life in three areas.

In the **physical world**, take the "law" of gravity. It is a statement about what we observe to be true related to two bodies in space: they are attracted to each other. Scientific laws like this are easy to understand and communicate.

The second type of law is found in the **moral realm**. Relating back to our study of Ethics, God has designed our day-to-day lives and relationships to work according to certain rules. The Ten Commandments are a prime example of this type of "law." What would the world be like if everyone observed the law to "love God" completely, or "not steal"? Let's face it, the world really does go better when we obey God's moral rules.

It becomes a little more difficult for students to grasp the idea of "law" as it relates to the **civil arena**. As we saw last week in our study of "Sociology," God has established the state to be responsible for administering His law on the level of society. In this sense, legislators do not "make up" laws, but their task is to move God's principles from the moral realm into the civil code. Therefore, all civil laws are based on religious ideas. This gives a whole different slant to the current misunderstanding of the idea of "separation of church and state." From this perspective, it is impossible to separate religious ideas from good government. This concept will be discussed further next week in the study of Politics.

"Natural law" was the phrase developed in the 1700's to describe how God has designed certain laws into the nature of things, whether physical, moral, or civil. It became the bedrock upon which the founders of our nation built a new form of civil government which became the United States of America. Although not a perfect place, our nation is a land of freedom and opportunity unprecedented in the history of mankind.

Regardless of the area (physical, moral or civil), laws are designed for our good. We should see them as good and seek to cooperate with them. If not, we can expect negative consequences.

key concept: Jesus Christ is Lawgiver.

key verse: Genesis 49:10:
"**The scepter will not depart from Judah, nor the ruler's staff (lawgiver) from between his feet, until he comes to whom it belongs and the obedience of the nations is his.**"

objectives: By the end of this lesson, each student should be able to

FOR THE REVIEW SESSION: SOCIOLOGY

. . . contrast how our society views the family with the biblical model.

. . . state a specific course of action for being "Salt and Light" in society.

FOR NEW TOPIC: LAW

. . . understand that God has established laws to govern the universe.

. . . describe the difference between physical law, moral law, and civil law.

. . . make a commitment to obey God's laws.

read: U.T.T., Chapter 30, Biblical Christian Law.

before class:

FOR THE REVIEW SESSION: SOCIOLOGY

☐ Make a copy for each student of the handout, "**My Christian Worldview of Sociology**" and have a pencil for each student.

☐ Gather articles from the daily paper related to social issues to use for discussion.

FOR NEW TOPIC: LAW

☐ Make 3 copies of "**The Molasses Kid Skit**" and enlist three students to play the parts in the skit of George, Harry, and Chris.

☐ Make one copy for each student of the handouts, "**The Nature of Law**" and "**Why Should We Obey God's Law.**" Also, have a pencil for each student.

PART ONE: REVIEW SOCIOLOGY

1. REVIEW: Begin with a short review/overview from last week's lesson. You may summarize or ask several students to share one thing they recall from the study on Sociology.

2. DISCUSS the following quote by writing it on the board or overhead: Man "is not a cog in a machine," says Francis A. Schaeffer, "he is not a piece of theater; he really can influence history. From the biblical viewpoint, man is lost, but great." (UTT, p. 227) **What does this imply about the nature of man (psychology)? With that in view, what does it imply about man and society? In other words, does man shape society, or does society shape man? What does Schaeffer mean when he says that "man is lost, but great"?**

3. "FAMILY" DISCUSSION: **A major building block of society is the family. How does our society today present a picture of marriage and the family?** Have a discussion on how school textbooks/curricula, movies, and TV portray the "family." List the various aspects on the left-hand side of the board. Summarize the list by having students come up with a short definition of "family" according to current standards. Then critique each item from a biblical worldview. Use the following biblical definition of "family" in their critique: one man + one woman + together for life + children = a family. Help students see the difference between the "ideal" and the "real." The fact that people come from broken families, etc, does not negate the biblical "ideal" definition of family as a goal for which society should strive.

4. DISCUSSION ON CHANGING OUR CULTURE: ASK: **Do you think that we, as Christians, can have an influence on our culture?** (Various answers) SAY: **Listen as I read an excerpt from Chuck Colson's *BreakPoint* series, and then we will discuss the implications for our society:**

    "In a new book, author Paul Corby Finney, a University of Missouri historian and archaeologist, sheds new light on the art of the early church and how Christians used artistic expression to transform their culture. . . . For example, signet rings were widely used in Roman times as official signatures for documents. The rings were pressed into the hot wax which sealed a paper scroll. The problem was that the rings commonly sold in the marketplaces typically had artistic representations of idols, homosexual lovers, and prostitutes all of which are contrary to Christian belief and practice. The early church father, Clement of Alexandria, instructed believers to purchase rings that reflected Christian virtues. That meant erotica was out. And since Christians are sober and peace-loving, said Clement, they should stay away from wine cups and weapons. Rather, they should choose seals depicting the ancient Christian symbol of the fish or doves, ships, or other representations that could be given a Christian meaning. Finney notes that as the church expanded, signet ring makers discovered less demand for erotica and a growing market for fish emblems. The cultural interaction on the part of Christians was reflected in the gradual transformation of pagan culture. They were not seeking to create a separate culture. They were Christianizing the culture they had."

    a. DISCUSS:
        1) **What eventually happened to the Roman empire?** (It turned from paganism and embraced Christianity.)

thinking like a christian

2) **Like the early Christians, how can we use the power of the marketplace to influence our culture and function as salt and light?** Let the discussion carry on, guiding students to think specifically about what they actually can do to change attitudes of their peers, teachers, community leaders, etc.

b. Don't allow the discussion to stop at vague generalities such as "Take a stand for Jesus." Ask them **"How, specifically, can you take a stand for Jesus in that situation?"**

c. You may want to note some of the suggestions, ask for commitments to be involved, and then follow-up in the coming weeks by asking how they are doing. Make it a point of prayer. Also, think through how you can make a difference in your world. Share those ideas with your group. Have them pray for you and hold you accountable for action and reporting back how you have taken a stand, and ask them to hold each other accountable as well!

5. DISCUSS NEWSPAPER ARTICLES: Ask if anyone has an article on social issues that he would like to share with the rest of the group. Pass out articles that you collected and have students read one at a time and discuss how the article relates to a biblical worldview.

6. HAND OUT the copies of "**My Christian Worldview on Sociology**" and help them fill in the blanks. The paragraph should read as follows:

"My Christian worldview of sociology states that God has ordained three social institutions where Christian relationships operate. These are: the **home,** the **church,** and the **state**. The **Bible** is the source of information to answer the question: "How can we build a **healthy** society?" The **family** is established as a **lifelong** relationship in which the husband and wife love and **serve** each other and raise children who know God's love and **truth.** The church functions as a body with **Christ** as the Head. The state functions to protect the **innocent** from the wrongdoer. Each one of these parts of society owes its existence to the **will** of God. Application of **biblical** principles to the **problems** of society give us solid solutions!"

PART TWO: NEW TOPIC: LAW

I. INTRODUCTION:

A. THE MOLASSES KID SKIT: Introduce the skit by saying: **Today we are going to start with a skit and discuss some of the ideas found in it. Listen carefully to what is said by each of the characters. We will discuss each of the characters afterwards.**

1. ASK the three students whom you enlisted for the skit to come to the front of the room. You read the part of the "Narrator" to begin and end the skit. After the skit, have the characters remain standing in front of the class as you ask the following questions to the class:

a. STAND beside Harry and ask: **What was Harry's perspective?** (It's O.K. as long as you are sincere. You can choose what's best for you.)

b. STAND beside Chris and ask: **What was Chris's perspective?** (There is a design built into the nature of things which needs to be followed.)

c. STAND beside George and ask: **If the skit continued, what do you anticipate would happen to George's car?** (George's engine would overheat, break down, etc.) **Why do you know this would happen?** (We know how engines are designed.)

thinking like a christian

d. ASK: **Whose perspective is better?** (Chris's) **Why?** (It fits reality.)

e. THANK the actors and have them sit down.

B. DISCUSS: **How is your life like the car engine in this skit?** (An engine is made to work in a certain way. It runs better with oil; it's not designed to run on molasses. In the same way, life is designed to work best in a certain way, to be lived according to God's design.)

C. TRANSITION: **Like a gasoline engine, "life" is designed to work in a certain way, too. That design built into life we call "law." The laws that make up the design of life are evident on three different levels. Today, we are going to explore the nature of these laws of life.**

II. THE NATURE OF LAW

A. PHYSICAL LAW: Give to each student a pencil and a handout, **"The Nature of Law"** as you SAY: **Everyone take a pencil and a handout. God has woven His LAW into the fabric of our world. What are these laws and how do we find out about them? The first type of law is PHYSICAL LAW. These are the laws that govern the physical world around us. The Bible indicates that God created the world and life and established these laws.** Have two students read each of the following passages: Genesis 1:14,21,24,27-28 and Colossians 1:15-17.

1. DISCUSS: **Give me an illustration of a physical law.** Have several students offer illustrations. (The law of gravity, the law of planetary motion, the laws of thermodynamics, the laws of heredity, the law of cause and effect, etc.)

2. ASK: **How do we find out about these laws?** (By studying nature, the physical world.)

3. ASK: **What do we call someone who studies these laws?** (Scientist.)

4. ASK: **Do these laws change?** (No.)

5. ASK: **What happens when you go against these laws?** (You suffer the consequences. If you walk off a tall building, you fall and go "boom." There are always consequences to breaking God's physical laws.)

6. TRANSITION: **The second type of law that God has designed into our world is called...**

B. **MORAL LAW: This relates to how we are to live before God and other people. Can you think of an illustration of a moral law?** Have several share an illustration. (Love God, do not murder, lie, steal, etc.) Have someone read Exodus 20:1-17 and someone else read Leviticus 18:1-5 and a third person read Romans 2:14-15.

1. ASK: **How do we find out about these laws?** (by studying the Bible) **Remember from our study of ethics that the moral laws in the Bible are really a reflection of what?** (The character of God.)

2 ASK: **The one who studies the moral laws as revealed in the character of God is called a what?** (A theologian.)

3. ASK: **Do these moral laws change?** (No.)

4. DISCUSS: **What happens when you go against these laws?** (You suffer the consequences.) **For example, if you steal, what might be the consequences?** (Allow discussion: you feel guilty, you might get caught and put in jail, God will call you into account, etc. There are always consequences to breaking God's moral laws.)

5. TRANSITION: **Besides these two types of laws, there is a third kind that we call...**

C. **CIVIL LAW: This relates to the principles that apply to our living together as a community or nation.** Have a different person read each of the following passages: Genesis 9:6 and Romans 13:1-5.

1. ASK: **Can you think of an illustration of a civil law?** (The speed limit posted on the highways, laws concerning marriage and divorce, the building code, etc.)

2. ASK: **How do we find out about these laws?** (By studying the world and the Word. Both areas of study help us to make good civil laws.)

3. ASK: **What do we call someone who studies civil law?** (A legislator: meaning one who "moves" the law. A legislator does not create or make up civil laws any more than a scientist makes up scientific laws. He discovers the laws that are already built into the fabric of the universe by God and "moves" those principles into the civil law code.)

   a. NEWTON ILLUSTRATION: **As a scientist, Sir Isaac Newton discovered the law of gravity. The law was already there. He just described it and studied it, so that the law could be used to help mankind.**

   b. SAY: **In the same way, the role of a legislator is to study the physical and moral laws as found in nature and the Bible, and then move them into the realm of civil law codes of society.**

4. ASK: **Do these laws change?** (Yes and no. Draw out this answer from the group and help them to think it through.) **Some laws change, like the speed limit. Other laws that are based on God's moral law should not change.**

   a. ASK: **Can you think of a civil law that should not change?** (Various answers: the marriage laws, laws against pornography, incest, homosexuality, etc.)

   b. DISCUSS: **What is the difference between these two types of laws; in other words, why should these laws not change?** (Because they are based on God's moral law that, like His character, does not change and is true for all people, in all places, at all times.) **This relates to our study of Ethics!**

5. ASK: **What happens when you go against these laws?** (You may suffer the consequences. If you are caught for exceeding the speed limit, you pay a fine. There are consequences to breaking the laws of government.)

thinking like a christian

III. WHY SHOULD WE OBEY GOD'S LAWS?

A. GIVE every student the second handout, **"Why Should We Obey God's Laws?"** as you SAY: **Now let's see how this applies to your life. On this second handout, let's read together ROMANS 2:16 -** "This will take place on the day when God will judge men's secrets through Jesus Christ, as my gospel declares." **Take a minute to answer the question on your sheet: "What will take place one day in the future?"** Allow a minute for writing, then ASK: **Who would like to share what you wrote?** (God will judge every person.)

B. SAY: **Now, follow as I read this next verse: ACTS 17:31 -** "For he has set a day when he will judge the world with justice by the man he has appointed. He has given proof of this to all men by raising him from the dead." **Take a minute to answer the question on your sheet: "How do we know that there will be a future judgment?"** Allow a minute for writing, then ASK: **Who would like to share what you wrote?** (because Jesus was raised from the dead)

C. SAY: **Let's read the last verse: 2 CORINTHIANS 5:10 -** "For we must all appear before the judgment seat of Christ, that each one may receive what is due him for the things done while in the body, whether good or bad." **Based on this verse, at the judgment, what will be received?** (justice: see the phrase "receive what is due" plus Acts 17:31 - "he will judge...with justice.") **What does "justice" mean?** (God will be completely fair and judge us according to His righteous standard.) **Does this remind you of our study of Theology and Ethics?** (Yes, God is righteous and commands us to obey His ethical law.)

IV. GENERAL APPLICATION

A. WRITE: **Take three minutes to think about what we have just read from the Bible and write a summary statement about why we should obey God's laws.** After three minutes ASK: **Who would like to share their summary?** (Various answers: God is just and will judge every person according to how they have obeyed His laws. Therefore, we should be careful to obey his moral and civil laws, or else suffer the consequences.)

B. READ the QUOTE at the bottom of the handout: **"Without a notion of a law-maker, it is impossible to have a notion of a law, and an obligation to observe it." John Locke, an English political writer of the 1700's, wrote that.**

   1. THEOLOGY: ASK: **What connection does Locke make between the idea of a lawmaker, the law, and obeying the law?** (The three ideas are interwoven. There is no such thing as a law without a lawmaker. Therefore, God is essential in order to have any laws, whether physical laws, moral laws, or civil laws.) ASK: **This relates to what worldview category?** (Theology) Go over to the worldview bulletin board and point to that piece of the puzzle.

   2. BIOLOGY: **How does law relate to our study of Biology?** (God created the world and life to operate according to set laws. All living things operate according to God's laws built into nature.)

   3. PSYCHOLOGY AND SOCIOLOGY: **What does our understanding of the nature of mankind (Psychology) tell us about man's ability to obey the moral and civil law?** (We tend not to obey either area. That is why we need the state (Sociology) to enforce the civil law by punishing the wrong-doer.

4. ETHICS: **Law relates to Ethics in what way?** (As we study the Bible to discern the moral absolutes for ethical conduct, we then move those moral standards into the realm of civil law so that we might have a more peaceful, free and orderly society.)

C. SUMMARY: **It's amazing how all of these parts fit together to make a seamless whole. Christianity is not concerned just about your personal, private relationship with God. It involves the totality of reality. It informs how you should live your life in every area you can imagine. It is a total world and life view. There is no escaping the implications of the Bible for every relationship and every idea in your life. God has it all covered!**

D. TRANSITION: **Do you see that this is too good to keep to ourselves? People all around you, your friends, do not realize these truths that we have been discussing each week.**

V. SPECIFIC APPLICATION: TAKE IT TO YOUR WORLD

A. FRIEND ILLUSTRATION: **What would you do if one of your best friends told you that he was going to jump off the top of a tall building?** (Tell him not to do it, try to keep him from doing it.)

1. ASK: **Why would you do that?** (because he will be killed and you love your friend)

2. ASK: **Why would he be killed?** (because of the law of gravity)

3. ASK: **So, because you know something about the real world and the laws that run it, that knowledge can save a life! A fall like that can just about ruin a guy's day!**

B. DISCUSSION QUESTION: **In the same way, when you see a friend breaking a moral law of God, your knowledge of that law can save him or her from ruining his life. Yet, while we don't hesitate to tell a friend not to jump off a building, we often have difficulty telling a friend that God's moral laws are the only way to go.**

1. ASK: **Why is this?** (Various answers.) You may pursue this line of thinking with a short discussion, helping them see the seriousness of sharing what they are learning in a loving, sensitive way with their friends, and the utter stupidity of allowing a friend to live a destructive life-style of pre-marital sex, illegal drugs, rebellion toward parents, jealousy toward successful classmates, etc.

2. DIGGING DEEPER: ASK: **What can you do this week to help someone understand something about the real world?** Encourage them to be specific about their application. You may ask probing questions such as: **Think of specific people you know. What do they need? What can you tell them to help them understand reality? When can you tell them? Who in our class will pray with you about talking to this person? Will you tell us next week how it went?** This last question will give a sense of accountability. Remember, people do what we INSPECT, not what we EXPECT. If you say all of this in love, students will not see you as badgering them,

thinking like a christian

but helping them to do what they already know they ought to do. And after they follow through, the angels will sing; and you and the rest of the class can rejoice in how God used them in the lives of their friends!

C. CLOSE the lesson by having the class stand in a circle, holding hands. Ask each person to say a sentence prayer thanking God for one aspect of His law: physical, moral, or civil. Also, encourage them to pray for one of their friends who does not understand how the world is run by God's laws.

D. NEXT WEEK: SAY: Next week we will review our study of Law and see how it has laid the foundation for our nation, the United States of America. During the week, look for articles or cartoons that deal with our political system. Pray every day for your friends who don't have a clue about the real world. God can use you to show them the way, the truth, and the life through Jesus' love and forgiveness!

"the molasses kid" skit

Narrator: George is standing beside his car with the hood up and a jar of molasses in his hand when Harry and Chris walk up.

Harry: "Hey, George, what are you doing?"

George: "I'm putting molasses into my engine to make it run better."

Harry: "That's cool. I mean, I've never tried it in my car, but as long as you're sincere about it, it's O.K. with me."

Chris: "Wait a minute, George. You are putting the molasses in the crankshaft where the oil is supposed to go. Engines are designed to run with oil, not molasses."

George: "Yeah, but this is a Chevy."

Chris: "That doesn't matter. Car engines are basically all the same. They all run on oil."

Harry: "Chris, let George do what he wants. Who are you to decide what's right for him. I'm not one to tell someone how to live his life."

Chris: "Look, you don't have to take my word for it. George, look in the glove compartment and read the owner's manual."

George: "O.K. Let's see, page 25, under 'Engine Care' it says in bold print, 'Use oil - do not use molasses.'"

Harry: "But hold on, George. Whose car is this? It's your car, right? Those guys don't know what's best for you. You should be able to do what you want to with your own car!"

George: "Yeah. I agree with Harry. It's my car. I bought it with my own money. I pay for the gas to run it. And I'm putting molasses in the engine! Molasses is sweet, and I like it on my pancakes in the morning. So that settles it."

Narrator: So George puts in the molasses, starts his engine, and drives off down the road.

"the molasses kid"

the nature of law

God has woven His LAW into the fabric of our world. What are these laws and how do we find out about them?

1. _____ **Law:** Genesis 1:14,21,24,27-28 and Colossians 1:15-17.

   Illustration:

   How do we find out about these laws?

   One who studies these laws is called a _____.

   Do these laws change?

   What happens when you go against these laws?

2. _____ **Law:**   Exodus 20:1-17, Leviticus 18:1-5, Romans 2:14-15.

   Illustration:

   How do we find out about these laws?

   One who studies these laws is called a _____.

   Do these laws change?

   What happens when you go against these laws?

3. _____ **Law:** Genesis 9:6; Romans 13:1-5.

   Illustration:

   How do we find out about these laws?

   The one who studies these laws is called a _____.

   Do these laws change?

   What happens when you go against these laws?

why should we obey God's laws?

ROMANS 2:16 - "This will take place on the day when God will judge men's secrets through Jesus Christ, as my gospel declares."

What will take place one day in the future?

ACTS 17:31 - "For he has set a day when he will judge the world with justice by the man he has appointed. He has given proof of this to all men by raising him from the dead."

How do we know that there will be a future judgment?

2 CORINTHIANS 5:10 - "For we must all appear before the judgment seat of Christ, that each one may receive what is due him for the things done while in the body, whether good or bad."

At the judgment, what will be received?

Write a summary statement about why you should obey God's laws:

SUMMARY: "Without a notion of a law-maker, it is impossible to have a notion of a law, and an obligation to observe it."
- John Locke, English political writer of the 1700's

My Christian
WORLDVIEW
of Sociology

My Christian worldview of sociology states that God has ordained three social institutions where Christian

relationships operate: the_____, the _____, and the _____. The_____is

the source of information which answers the question: "How can we build a _____society?" The

_____is established as a _____relationship in which husband and wife love and

_____each other and raise children who know God's love and _____. The church functions

as a body with _____as its Head. The state functions to protect the _____ from the

wrongdoer. Each one of these parts of society owes its existence to the _____ of God. Application of

_____principles to the _____of society gives us solid solutions!

notes & ideas

overview
lesson 9

politics: what about government?

*There are two things that should not be discussed
in polite company: religion and politics.*

Is that "saying," true? By now you've come to realize that religion is the basis for everything; all categories of a worldview begin with religious ideas and beliefs. "Politics" is the topic of this week's lesson, so we'll just have to dive in with both feet and hope that the "polite company" will understand!

When it comes to this subject, many of your students will wonder why they should study "politics" in church or a Bible study. They likely will think that politics is "dirty" and conjure up ideas of corrupt politicians, government waste in this country, and abusive governments throughout history and in other parts of the world today.

Yet, mankind cannot get along without some form of political structure. According to our study of "Sociology," the state ("politics") is one of the social institutions ordained by God and necessary for maintaining a free and orderly society. Our political structure in particular requires that each citizen be informed about the principles of civil government. A nation built on the principles of individual liberty and responsibility can be sustained only when the majority of citizens are aware and involved in the political process. That is why this lesson is so strategic.

Likewise, this lesson is crucial because the <u>biblical</u> principles of politics are not studied in our public schools and colleges today. These important principles that are the foundation of our entire system of government must be taught through our churches and homes.

Your challenge this week is to communicate clearly the vital role that Biblical Christianity has played in the area of civil government. The group lesson helps you achieve this goal as the "Review" session examines the biblical concepts that are evident in the *Declaration of Independence,* our nation's founding document. Students are then introduced to various types of government, from a monarchy to a democratic republic. This helps them to think about the important principles that go into forming a government that is good for the people.

During the "Bible search" section, your group will be surprised at the number of biblical principles that relate to government. And finally, they will be challenged to take a positive role in our political system in order to fulfill their God-given responsibility as citizens in a free society.

NOTE: You may have some questions about the interface between "religion and politics." In addition to the chapters on "Biblical Christian Politics" and "Secular Humanist Politics" in *Understanding the Times,* another excellent source is *Original Intent: The Courts, The Constitution, & Religion,* by David Barton, published in 1996 and available from WallBuilder Press, (817) 441-6044.

key concept: Jesus is King of Kings and Lord of Lords.

key verse: Revelation 19:16:
"On his robe and on his thigh he has his name written: KING OF KINGS AND LORD OF LORDS."

objectives: By the end of this lesson, each student should be able to

FOR THE REVIEW SESSION: LAW

. . . describe the concept of "natural law" and how it is the basis for our system of government as set out in the *Declaration of Independence.*

. . . apply the principles learned in this and earlier lessons to the current issues of abortion, homosexuality, pornography, murder, etc.

FOR NEW TOPIC: POLITICS

. . . discuss the purpose of government according to the Bible and trace those biblical principles in the founding of our republic.

. . . define his role as a citizen of "two kingdoms."

read: U.T.T., Chapter 34, Biblical Christian Politics.

before class:

FOR THE REVIEW SESSION: LAW

☐ Make a copy for each student of each handout, **"The Declaration of Independence"** and **"My Christian Worldview of Law."**

☐ Have a pencil or pen for each student.

FOR NEW TOPIC: POLITICS

☐ Take the pages on different forms of government from the end of this lesson and post them at eye-level in various locations around the room.

☐ Make a copy for each student of the handout, **"Ben Franklin at the Constitutional Convention," "The Bible on Politics,"** & **"Politics and You."**

☐ Have a pencil for each student.

☐ A suggestion for the closing prayer time is to gather the names of elected officials on the local, state, and national level. Post them or type them to hand out and have students pray for them by name.

PART ONE: REVIEW LAW

1. SHARING:

    a. ASK if anyone had the opportunity during the week to share about the reality of life with one of their friends. Have him relate what was said and how it went.

    b. ASK if anyone has a political cartoon to show the class. Discuss the artist's point of view and the worldview implications of the cartoon.

2. NATURAL LAW: SAY: **Last week we learned about laws. Laws are simply descriptions of the nature of things. During the 1700's, men began to write about these laws that are discerned in nature as "natural laws."**

    a. WORLDVIEW: Write "natural law" on the board, then go over to the worldview bulletin board puzzle and point to the different pieces as you SAY: **Natural law is based on the idea that God (that's our Theology) created the universe (Biology) separate from Himself (this relates to Philosophy) to work in certain ways (there's Law) and these ways can be known by man (like we learned in Psychology). Man can use his reason to understand these laws of nature.**

    b. REVIEW: **The laws that describe the nature of things are divided into three categories. Can you recall from last week those three categories?** (Physical laws: like the law of gravity. Moral laws: like do not steal. Civil laws: like punishment for an evil doer.)

    c. TRANSITION: **This week, we are going to see how this understanding of the laws of nature, or "natural law," forms the basis for our civil government.**

3. NATURAL LAW AND THE FOUNDING OF OUR COUNTRY

    a. DECLARATION OF INDEPENDENCE: **Natural law played a major role in the early development of the United States of America. One of the founding documents of our country, "The Declaration of Independence," provides for us a blueprint of this relationship.**

        1) AGREE/DISAGREE: **I am going to make a statement that I want you either to agree or disagree with. The statement is this: "The Declaration of Independence is a religious as well as a political document." If you agree with that, stand up and move over to the right side of the room. If you dis agree, stand over to the left side of the room. If you are not sure, stand in the middle of the room.** Repeat the statement and have everyone move to one point in the room.

        2) DISCUSS: Lead a discussion on the students' positions about the statement. Draw out their reasons without adding a lot of your own at this point. This exercise is just to get them thinking. Take 3 or 4 minutes on this, have them return to their seats, and then move on to the next section.

3) SUMMARY: **Thanks for your ideas. In order to answer whether the Declaration is religious or just political, we need to take a look at what the document actually says. In that way, we will allow the writers and signers of the Declaration to express for themselves what they were thinking at the time.**

4) TRANSITION: **The Declaration was written as the official statement of the founding fathers, telling the nations of the world why the colonies in America were seeking to be free from British rule. To see if the founders were resting their case on religious ideas, let's find out what the basis of those reasons were.**

b. INDIVIDUAL STUDY: Give each student a copy of the handout, **"THE DECLARATION OF INDEPENDENCE"** and a pencil. Have them circle any references or ideas that relate to a belief in God. GIVE THEM 4 MINUTES FOR THIS ACTIVITY.

c. GROUP DISCUSSION: After four minutes, **LEAD A DISCUSSION** on what they circled and why. You can draw out the following ideas during the discussion. However, KEEP IT BRIEF AND TO THE POINT OR TIME WILL GET AWAY.

1) "LAWS OF NATURE": This alternate term for "natural law" points to God's involvement in providing guidelines, not only for moral behavior, but also for living in society. This concept of natural law was studied in our law schools across America and formed the basis for our entire legal system until the last 20 to 30 years. In more recent years, law students have studied "positive" law, which is based on the ideas of man, not the principles of God.

2) "NATURE'S GOD": This phrase refers to the God of the Bible, not the god of Buddhism, Islam, or any other religion. The majority of the founders were Christian theists; in fact 52 out of 55 belonged to churches of various Christian denominations. They believed that God reveals Himself and His truth in three ways: through the natural world, through the Bible, and ultimately through Jesus Christ, as the Word Incarnate (in the flesh). The Laws of Nature and Nature's God reflect the founders' worldview understanding of Philosophy and Theology.

3) "TRUTHS TO BE SELF-EVIDENT": Truth relates to the absolute truth based on the Bible. "Self-evident" means that it is clear for all people everywhere to see. See Romans 1:20. There is no such thing as truth apart from Jesus and the Bible.

4) "ALL MEN ARE CREATED EQUAL": Mankind is the special creation of the God of the Bible and are created in God's image (Psychology). All humans are equal in God's sight and before the law, although all people do not possess equal abilities, intelligence, etc.

NOTE: A student may raise the issue of SLAVERY, saying that the founders did not view slave as equal to free white men. The issue of slavery goes beyond the scope of the main point of this lesson. You may respond briefly by saying that while some of the delegates were slave holders, most were not. The point for this lesson is that a consistent biblical worldview holds that all people are created equal in God's sight. The fact that all the founders did not live up to that standard in their personal practice underscores the biblical view that man is basically sinful and does not always live up to God's standards. We would rightly judge those slave-holders for not acting according to the biblical principle of creation. Later, this issue of slavery came under heated debate during the writing of the constitution, where many of the delegates to the constitutional

thinking like a christian

convention did not want to allow slavery in the union of states. Gouverneur Morris stated that slavery was ". . . the curse of heaven on the States where it prevailed. . ." and he referred to slavery as a "defiance of the most sacred laws of humanity." A compromise was reached with the southern states to allow the importation of slaves until the year 1808, after which time Congress could pass laws forbidding the practice. In addition, according to the Northwest Ordinance, any new states added to the union were required to be "free" states, not allowing slavery. Also, remember that slavery was finally abolished by four Christian statesmen - David Livingston, Henry Stanley, Gordon of Khartoum, and William Wilberforce.

5) "CREATOR": The Creator God of the Bible, who has "endowed" mankind with certain rights. Since God made the world and mankind, He has the right to establish the rules by which to live. This is part of the founders' Biology. They had a worldview!

6) "UNALIENABLE RIGHTS": This is a very important concept. These rights about to be enumerated, i.e., life, liberty, and the pursuit of happiness (including private property), were basic rights because they are given by God. That made these rights unalienable. That is, they cannot be taken away by any man or government except by due process of law. God is a higher authority than men or governments.

7) "LIFE": The right to one's life and person is basic to all law. No one has the right to take another's life because that right is reserved to God alone. Only in certain circumstances does God delegate that right to the people. See Genesis 9:6. This forfeiture of life requires due process of law.

   a) DISCUSS: **ASK: What implications for the abortion issue do you perceive in this most basic right?** Allow the group to wrestle with this issue with a short discussion.

   b) RESPOND TO their ideas like this: An unborn child is innocent and his/her life should not be taken away, even by a law passed by Congress, because there is a higher law of God that is unalienable. The so-called "mother's right" is beside the point! Other issues, such as the health of the mother is, more often than not, also beside the point. It is only in the rarest of cases that a mother is in danger of death from her pregnancy.

      NOTE: Don't allow the discussion to get into a full-fledged debate on the issue of abortion. Again, the point here is to establish the fact that the founders' understanding of life, their worldview, came from a biblical understanding of reality. Therefore, they would have been horrified at the prospect of abortion, since it takes the life of an innocent victim.

8) "LIBERTY": This means the freedom to choose one's course in life, but only within the boundaries of the moral framework of the Bible. That is why our study of biblical Ethics is important.

   a) DISCUSS: ASK: **What implications for the rights of homosexuals do you perceive in this concept of liberty?** Allow a short discussion.

thinking like a christian

lesson 9

b) DRAW A CIRCLE on the board to represent God's moral standards. Write inside the circle terms like, "love," "serve others," "help the poor," "sexual intimacy inside of marriage," etc. These are the things that God desires for us to do. Outside these moral boundaries, write terms like "hate," "murder," "steal," "sex outside of marriage." Stress that God has set boundaries for our moral behavior. We have liberty to practice anything inside that border. It's like playing football; you have to stay within the sidelines to play the game!

c) RESPOND TO their ideas like this: Homosexuality is clearly contrary to God's commands and principles found in the Bible; see 1 Corinthians 6:9-11 for starters. It is outside the boundaries of biblical Ethics. Therefore, it is not a "right" as envisioned by the founding fathers. Refer back to the study of Sociology where the Bible defines the "family" as one man with one women for life. God created Adam and Eve, not Adam and Steve! 1 Cor. 6:11 states that such behaviors as homosexuality were practiced by some of the Corinthians. The emphasis is on the "were." They no longer practiced those things because they had been washed clean in the blood of Jesus Christ.

9) "PURSUIT OF HAPPINESS": This right is similar to that of "Liberty." One is only free to pursue happiness within the framework of biblical morals. It might make you happy to kill your neighbor, but that is not a "right" that God gives you to pursue. The Bible says, "Do not murder." God established government to punish those who go outside the boundaries of biblical ethics.

10) "SUPREME JUDGE OF THE WORLD": God is not only the Creator of the world, He is also Judge. Refer back to last week's lesson. This means that He has established standards of conduct by which to live. And it also means that He will bring an account for how we live our lives. He not only judges men individually, He also judges the conduct of nations. All the Old Testament is the history of God judging nations, including the nation of Israel.

11) "DIVINE PROVIDENCE": Another characteristic of God is His "providence," which means His daily working out of His will on earth. God is involved in the day-to-day activities of His people. ASK: **How is this different from the Deist concept of God?** (The biblical concept is that God is Creator and made the world; and He is still around to oversee mankind's conduct. The Deist concept is that God created the world but has left it to run on its own and no longer interferes with human matters.)

d. ASK: **What do you say about my original question? Is the Declaration both a religious and a political document?** (YES, it is totally based on a religious worldview and it sets out a definite political action, i.e. separating from England for specific reasons as specified in the document.)

e. SUMMARY: **So we can see from this document that the founding of our nation was based on biblical principles, specifically the idea of natural law. The men who ratified this Declaration were serious about what they had put down, because they were declaring war on the most powerful nation on earth. They pledged their property, their honor, and their lives by signing this document. They were willing to die for the truth on which they based their lives.**

f. TRANSITION: **Since the founding of our country was based on a biblical world view, we will now consider how that worldview relates to the unique political structure that our founders established for our nation.**

PART TWO: NEW TOPIC: POLITICS

I. INTRODUCTION:

A. PROJECT MARS: **The year is 2095. We are presently in a spaceship traveling to Mars. Our mission is to start a new colony on that planet. The last 10 years on earth has seen international wars and almost total destruction of human life. For that reason, we are trying to start over again with a new civilization. Here in this room, you have been selected to choose our new system of government. Posted around the room are listed various forms of government that different nations have used throughout the history of life on earth. Study them carefully. Identify their strengths and their flaws. We must do better than our ancestors. We must form a government that will endure and not make the same mistakes of those who went before us. Use the next six minutes to study the documents around the room. Then we will convene to discuss your ideas.** After six minutes, call everyone back to their seats.

1. DISCUSS: **Let's pool our ideas and see if we can come up with an agreement as to how we should form our new government. Who wants to be first to suggest how we should start?** Lead a discussion for about 5-6 minutes. Ask probing questions such as: Why do you think that a democratic republic is the best way to go; What aspect of that form of government do you like the most; Do we need to modify it in some way; If so, in what way; How would this new government make laws; Would you have a judiciary; How are the judges selected; What would be their jurisdiction? Use the worldview ideas already discussed in previous lessons. Ask: How would that idea you just mentioned relate to what we know from biblical Psychology about the nature of man; How would we determine what are good laws; How do we insure that people obey the laws we pass?

    ANOTHER APPROACH would be to play "devil's advocate" by siding with a student who may promote a system of government that is unpopular with the rest of the class. Do this by high lighting some of the strengths of that system, such as the idea that in a monarchy, you could have a good, kind, and just king. Or, in communism, there is no need for anyone to steal, because everyone shares equally and no one owns anything privately!

    NOTE: Do not let this discussion go beyond 5-6 minutes. Do not expect to complete the assignment. The purpose is to start the process and to get everyone thinking about what elements are important to government and WHY each element is needed. Specific principles will be brought out during the rest of this lesson.

2. SUMMARY: **This has been a good discussion. It has made us think about the different elements necessary for good government. Also, we have raised some questions that we can answer only by reflecting on our worldview.**

thinking like a christian

B. TRANSITION: Let's come back to planet earth. Trying to decide on a system of government is tough to do. There are a lot of things to consider. A little over 200 years ago, a group of men sat down to write a new constitution. It led to the founding of our nation.

II. THE FOUNDING OF THE UNITED STATES

A. FRANKLIN QUOTE: Read aloud the article at the end of this lesson, "Ben Franklin at the Constitutional Convention." Then, hand out student copies of his speech and SAY: Take this copy of Franklin's speech. Circle each reference to a biblical worldview, and in the margin, list the worldview category that corresponds with it. For example, when he refers to the "Imperfection of the Human Understanding," Franklin acknowledges that mankind does not understand everything perfectly, indicating the biblical view of a fallen sin nature, which comes under which study? (Psychology.) Now you see what other references he makes, circle them and write in the margin one of the categories we've studied from our worldview puzzle. If you see something that he took right out of the Bible, put a square around that phrase. You may begin now. After a few minutes for writing, ask them to share what they found. Below are suggested answers.

1. PHILOSOPHY: "groping. . . to find political <u>truth</u>": The idea of truth is based on biblical Philosophy, that there is such a thing as "truth."

2. PSYCHOLOGY: "<u>groping</u>. . . to find political truth": Mankind has a rational mind that can comprehend the truth once it is discovered.

3. POLITICS: "groping. . . to find <u>political</u> truth": There is truth that applies to the realm of "politics."

4. LAW: "groping. . . to find <u>political truth</u>": This "political truth" that is being sought would be based on laws that are built into the nature of things, i.e. natural law.

5. THEOLOGY: "applying to the Father of lights...prayer...divine protection...powerful Friend...assistance...God governs in the affairs of men...etc." There is a personal (relational), all-powerful (ruler) God, who is involved in the lives and actions of all people. We must submit to His ways in order to be successful in this political exercise.

6. PHILOSOPHY: "Sacred writings" refers to the Bible. This answers the philosophical question: "How do I know what is true?". Franklin's answer is: "The Bible is sacred, i.e., sent from God Therefore, truth comes from the revealed Word of God.

7. SPARROW: "And if a sparrow cannot fall to the ground..." Jesus spoke these words in Matthew 10:29.

8. HOUSE: "Unless the Lord build the house..." This is found in Psalm 127:1.

9. BABEL: "we shall succeed...no better than the builders of Babel." This reference is to Genesis 11:8-9.

thinking like a christian

B. SUMMARY: You can see from this that our founding fathers, such as Ben Franklin, had a deep-seated understanding of how a biblical view relates to all of life. The political structure they were seeking to build rested firmly on a religious foundation. Because of this biblical worldview, how did Franklin apply it to their situation? (He suggested that they start every day in prayer for God's assistance.)

1. SAY: You can see from this that the worldview of these men influenced how they acted and what they designed for our government. By the way, the result of Franklin's call for prayer led to the entire delegation going to a local church the next morning to hear a sermon and a prayer by one of the pastors of that city. This changed the entire mood of the convention and resulted in the document that we now know as the Constitution of the United States. This is the only constitution in history that has lasted for over 200 years. By contrast, in the same 200 year period, France has gone through 8 different constitutions!

2. WHY SUCCESS?: ASK: But why do you think the founding fathers had such success in putting together this constitution? (Various answers.) These are good ideas. Primarily, they had success because they were basing their ideas of government on principles that correspond to the real world. In contrast, the French based their ideas for government on a humanist foundation that asserts there is no God and that mankind is basically good. The result was the French revolution, which ended in a blood bath and brought Napoleon to power as a military dictator to restore order!

C. TREE ILLUSTRATION: Draw a picture of a tree with its root system below the surface as you SAY: Think of it this way. Every tree has a root system that feeds and nourishes the entire plant. The fruit produced on the end of the branches comes as a natural result of the nourishment from the roots. The fruit is related organically to the roots. In other words, the roots determine the fruit! Got it?! Good!

1. POLITICAL FRUIT: Now follow along with what I am about to say. The delegates at the Constitutional Convention had the same task that we experienced a few minutes ago. They sat down with a blank sheet of paper and said, "What type of government should we make?" They were starting from scratch.

    a. THREE BRANCHES: John Adams refers to our form of government as a "democratical republic." (See *The Adams - Jefferson Letters*, published by The University of North Carolina Press (1987), p. 595.) An important component of our constitution is the design which called for three branches of government: the legislative, the executive, and the judicial. The founders didn't have to put in three branches, but they chose to do so. Why? (As a system of checks and balances, to keep one person or group of people from having too much power.)

    b. ASK: But why were the founders afraid of someone having too much power? (Because people might abuse their power and use it in a corrupt way.)

    c. ASK: Why were they afraid that someone in power might use their power in a corrupt way? (Because they had seen it happen before in history.) SAY: We still

lesson 9

thinking like a christian

are not at the root cause. **Why did the founders believe that people might abuse the power of government?** (Because of man's basic sin nature.) **Right! It's because of their religious understanding concerning the nature of man.**

2. RELIGIOUS ROOTS: Write the following words (in CAPS) beside the tree, starting at the roots and working your way up the trunk to the branches and to the fruit on the end of the branches as you SAY: **The founders' THEOLOGY** (roots), **that there is a God who sets the standards and to whom mankind is accountable, led to their PSYCHOLOGY** (trunk), **an understanding about human nature, which in turn fed their POLITICS** (branch), **a system of governing, which came out in the fruit of THREE BRANCHES OF GOVERNMENT** (fruit on the end of branch).

3. SUMMARY: **You cannot separate the root from the fruit. The roots of any system of government are always religious! You cannot separate religious ideas from political practice.**

D. ADAM'S QUOTE: **John Quincy Adams, our third president, said it this way: "The highest glory of the American Revolution was this; it connected in one indissoluble bond the principles of civil government with the principles of Christianity."** As you say this, hold both hands out in front of you and intertwine your fingers to illustrate a uniting of two things into an "indissoluble bond." **He is saying that these two things cannot be separated. They are linked together to make a whole, which is how our system of government is united with biblical ideas as written into the constitution.**

E. TRANSITION: **We saw from Franklin's speech that he was basing his ideas on the Bible. Adams said that our government is based on the principles of Christianity. So now let's find out what some of those principles are that come out of the Bible and give us a fuller understanding of the role and purpose of government.**

III. BIBLICAL PRINCIPLES OF POLITICS

A. HANDOUTS: Give to each student a handout, **"The Bible on Politics"** as you SAY: **On your handouts are several passages from the Bible that illustrate some of these principles. Read over the verses and answer the questions individually. Write any questions or comments you have in the margin, and we will discuss them. You have five minutes.**

1. GROUP DISCUSSION: Review the handout by leading a group discussion. Do this as time permits, being sure to leave time for PERSONAL APPLICATION.

2. SUMMARY: Close the discussion by asking how they might summarize in one sentence these biblical principles. Then read the suggested summary from your Teacher Copy.

B. APPLICATION: Give each student the handout, **"Politics and You"** as you SAY: **Some Christians have the idea that we should not be involved in politics. But in Matthew 22:15-22, Jesus refers to two kingdoms.** Have a volunteer read the passage, then ASK: **What are the two kingdoms Jesus mentions?** (Caesar, who rules the state, and God, who rules the entire world.) **Jesus is referring to the things that belong to God and the things that belong to the state. We must live in <u>both</u> kingdoms.**

1. EXAMPLE: WILBERFORCE: **Let me give you an example of a man who lived in both kingdoms. William Wilberforce was an English statesman who served in Parliament in the early 1800's. As a Christian, he believed that slavery was wrong, so he worked tirelessly in Parliament to abolish the slave trade in his country. It took him over 20 years, but he finally succeeded shortly before his death. Do you think it's important to be involved in politics today? Why or why not?** (Yes, because, like Wilberforce, Christians can have a positive influence on the laws that rule their country.)

2. RIGHTEOUS RULERS: SAY: **Look at the verse printed on your handout. Proverbs 29:2 says "When the righteous thrive, the people rejoice; when the wicked rule, the people groan."**

    a. ASK: **Can you think of specific examples of people rejoicing under a righteous ruler and groaning under a wicked ruler?** (Under Ronald Reagan, our country prospered economically, and his determination and policies helped to collapse the Soviet Union. Under Hitler, many people were murdered as he plunged the world into a great world-wide war. You may think of other examples.)

    b. ASK: **How would you apply this principle in our country, where we have the right to vote for our rulers?** (We should vote for people who demonstrate righteousness as well as political insight and wisdom.)

C. PERSONAL APPLICATION: SAY: **Take a minute to think about ways that you can apply the principles we discussed. Write down three or four things that come to mind.** Allow a few minutes for writing, then ask for volunteers to share what they wrote.

1. SUMMARY: You may summarize their responses or say the following: **One way for you to be involved politically is to run for office in your student government. This gives you first-hand experience in governing. Another thing you can do is to be involved in a local, state, or national campaign for help a godly candidate get elected to office. A third idea is to pray for those already in office. And, finally, you can stay informed about the issues before the legislature, and write letters to congressmen and your local or school paper concerning those issues.**

2. SAY: **Now, let's get specific. Pick one of the things on your list that you will definitely plan to do. Write out when you will do it, and the steps you will take to accomplish it.** After a few minutes of writing, ask for any volunteers to share their specific plans.

3. TABLE TALK: **The next chance you have, share with your parents some of the ideas we discussed today. Ask them how they are involved in our political system. Then ask them the questions listed under "Table Talk." This should be a lively discussion!**

D. CLOSE IN PRAYER: Suggestion: Post the names of local, state and national elected leaders or have them printed on a sheet to hand out. Have students pray for these officials by name during your closing prayer time.

thinking like a christian

The Declaration of Independence

In congress, July 4, 1776, the Unanimous Declaration
of the Thirteen United States of America

When in the Course of human events, it becomes necessary for one people to dissolve the political bands which have connected them with another, and to assume among the powers of the earth, the separate and equal station to which the Laws of Nature and of Nature's God entitles them, a decent respect to the opinions of mankind requires that they should declare the causes which impel them to the separation.

We hold these truths to be self-evident, that all men are created equal. That they are endowed by their Creator with certain unalienable rights, that among these are Life, Liberty and the pursuit of Happiness. That to secure these rights, governments are instituted among Men, deriving their just powers from the consent of the governed....

We, Therefore, the Representatives of the United States of America in General Congress, Assembled, appealing to the Supreme Judge of the world for the rectitude of our intentions.... And for the support of this Declaration, with a firm reliance on the protection of Divine Providence, we mutually pledge to each other our Lives, our Fortunes, and our sacred Honor.

the Bible on "politics"

EXODUS 18:13-23:

1. Jethro suggested that Moses organize different levels for what purpose? (A judicial system.)
2. What kind of men was Moses to appoint? (Godly men.)
3. Is this important for today? In what way? (Yes, because Godly men have a moral perspective on life.)

ISAIAH 33:22:

What are the three ways that God relates to mankind that parallel three ways our government is organized? (Judicial, Legislative, Executive branches.)

ROMANS 13:2-4:

1. From where does government get its authority? (From God.)
2. What is the role of government toward individuals? (To protect the one who does right and punish the one who does wrong. Note: "the sword" implies punishment by death.)

GENESIS 9:6:

1. What is established by the principles of verse 6? (God has delegated His authority to man [civil government] to administer justice [judicial system] by means of the death penalty for murder.)
2. Why did God give that principle? (A person's life is given by God, created in His image, and cannot be taken away by another man. This establishes the "right to life" as written in the *Declaration of Independence*.)

1 PETER 2:13-14:

What are two purposes of government? (To condemn the evil doer and protect the one who does right.)

AMOS 5:12, 15:

1. The court system is established to do what? (Promote justice.)
2. Why is that important? (It is based on the character of God. God is Just.)

EXODUS 23:1-6:

The specific examples listed here relate to what general principle? (Promoting justice and equity before the law.)

SUMMARY: Government is designed to . . .(Promote justice by protecting the innocent and restraining the evildoer.)

BEN FRANKLIN AT THE CONSTITUTIONAL CONVENTION

During the summer of 1787 in the city of Philadelphia, over 50 delegates met in the city's courthouse to design a government that would transform a loose assortment of states into a united nation. Eighty-one year old Benjamin Franklin rose to address George Washington, President of the Convention. He said:

Mr. President:

The small progress we have made after 4 or five weeks close attendance & continual reasoning with each other. . . is methinks a melancholy proof of the imperfection of the Human Understanding. . . .

In this situation of this Assembly, groping as it were in the dark to find political truth. . .how has it happened, Sir, that we have not hitherto once thought of humbly applying to the Father of lights to illuminate our understanding? In the beginning of the Contest with G. Britain, when we were sensible of danger we had daily prayer in this room for the divine protection.--Our prayers, Sir, were heard & they were graciously answered. . . . And have we now forgotten that powerful Friend? or do we imagine we no longer need his assistance? I have lived, Sir, a long time, and the longer I live, the more convincing proofs I see of this truth--that God Governs in the affairs of men. And if a sparrow cannot fall to the ground without his notice, is it probable that an empire can rise without his aid? We have been assured, Sir, in the sacred writings, that "except the Lord build the House, they labor in vain, that build it." I firmly believe this; and I also believe that without his concurring aid we shall succeed in this political building no better, than the Builders of Babel. . . .

I therefore. . . move--that henceforth prayers imploring the assistance of Heaven, and its blessing on our deliberations, be held in this Assembly every morning before we proceed to business, and that one or more of the clergy of this city be requested to officiate in that service.

(quoted in *The Myth of Separation*, David Barton, pp. 108-109.)

the Bible on "politics"

EXODUS 18:13-23:

1. Jethro suggested that Moses organize different levels for what purpose?

2. What kind of men was Moses to appoint?

3. Is this important for today? In what way?

ISAIAH 33:22:

What are the three ways that God relates to mankind that parallel three ways our government is organized?

ROMANS 13:2-4:

1. From where does government get its authority?

2. What is the role of government toward individuals?

GENESIS 9:6:

1. What is established by the principles of verse 6?

2. Why did God give that principle?

1 PETER 2:13-14:

What are two purposes of government?

AMOS 5:12, 15:

1. The court system is established to do what?

2. Why is that important?

EXODUS 23:1-6:

The specific examples listed here relate to what general principle?

SUMMARY: Government is designed to . . .

politics and you

living in two kingdoms:

In Matthew 22:15-22, Jesus refers to two spheres:

1.

2.

righteous rulers:

"When the righteous thrive, the people rejoice; when the wicked rule, the people groan."
(Proverbs 29:2)

how i can be involved. . .

1.

2.

3.

4.

table talk:

1. Should government pass legislation on moral issues?

2. When should you disobey the government?

3. What is meant by "separation of church and state"?

thinking like a christian

democratic republic

A government based upon a written constitution (covenant, contract) protecting it's citizens life, liberty and property. Citizens elect their representatives democratically with legislation based on a majority vote, implemented by an executive branch and judged constitutional by an impartial judiciary.

communism

A system of government in which the state establishes socialism* by means of force.

(*Socialism is an economic system based on the abolition of private property and focuses economic decisions in central planners.)

oligarchy

A government by a small group or class of people. This group or class is the ruling party over the rest of the citizens.

plutocracy

A government in which the wealthy rule. A wealthy class controls a government.

democracy

The form of govern-ment in which citizens hold the ruling power, so that the majority rules. All legislation is based on a majority vote.

monarchy

A king is the supreme ruler over the people. All authority rests with the king.

lesson 10

economics: what about money?

*"The subject which is normally considered boring was brought to life by your lesson plan. . . .
They had a ball doing the Melodrama."* A quote from a youth teacher who field tested this lesson.

Don't let this one scare you. At first glance, "economics" can seem like a topic that is either too technical for students or too removed from their day-to-day concerns. Nothing could be further from the truth.

Jesus talked more about money and how we use it than about any other single topic. And in our materialistic society, everybody thinks about money. . . how to earn it. . .how to spend it. . .and how to get more of it! So don't be misled; students definitely will be interested in this lesson on how the economy works!

However, the title, "Economics," can be an instant "turn-off" to many students. To overcome this problem, the introduction to the lesson plunges the class into a stimulating scenario that captures their attention and eases them into the topic in an interesting way. From there, you are off and running as they hear about a popular rock singer's personal struggle with money and meaning. Next, students dive into a rollicking melodrama which introduces the fundamentals of how and why we have money. From there it's time to cook up a recipe for "economic stew" that will leave them with biblical principles of economies!

So don't worry; this is nothing like your Economics 101 course in college! This lesson actually speaks to real life and offers practical ideas that form another piece of the worldview puzzle. Without this piece in place, students will enter the world with a hole in their biblical "understanding of the times."

key concept: Jesus Christ is the Owner.

key verse: I Corinthians 10:26:
"The earth is the Lord's and everything in it."

objectives: By the end of the session, students should be able to
FOR THE REVIEW SESSION: POLITICS
. . . state the connection between government and religion.
. . . know the relationship between personal liberty and trust in God.
. . . recognize the principle that truth does not change as it applies to every worldview category.

FOR NEW TOPIC: ECONOMICS
. . . understand how the basic concepts of a "free market" economy relate to biblical principles.
. . . make specific application in their lives of biblical principles for acquiring and using money.

read: U.T.T., Chapter 38, Biblical Christian Economics.

before class:
FOR THE REVIEW SESSION: POLITICS
☐ Have enough pennies for each student to have one.
☐ The quotes by Jay, Madison, and de Tocqueville can be written on the board, copied and handed out, or copied onto an overhead cell.
☐ Provide a copy of the handout titled, **"My Christian Worldview of Politics,"** and a pencil for each student.

FOR NEW TOPIC: ECONOMICS
☐ Each student should have a pencil and a copy of the handout, **"Shoes, Cows, and Economic Stew"** **(two pages).**

PART ONE: REVIEW POLITICS

1. DISCUSS the following quote by John Jay (1745-1829), Governor of the state of New York, president of the American Bible Society (1821) and appointed by George Washington as the first Chief Justice of the Supreme Court:

   "No human society has ever been able to maintain both order and freedom, both cohesiveness and liberty, apart from the moral precepts of the Christian Religion allied and accepted by all the classes. Should our Republic ere forget this fundamental precept of governance, men are certain to shed their responsibilities for licentiousness and this great experiment will surely be doomed." [1]

   a. ASK: Why does Jay call our nation a "great experiment"? (The kind of government they were creating had never been tried before in the history of mankind. It was an experiment to see if a freely elected government with limited powers would be enough to maintain justice, order and freedom in society and still allow individuals liberty to govern their own lives.)

   b. ASK: What does "licentiousness" mean? (Living immorally.)

   c. ASK: Do we see evidence of people shedding their responsibilities for licentiousness? In what ways? (Yes. Have students give specific answers from their own community, campus, or in the news, etc.)

   d. ASK: If the purpose of government is to maintain order, justice and freedom, then what is the connection between good government and religion? (The Christian religion is necessary if government is to allow people the greatest amount of freedom. If people do not govern themselves according to God's moral laws, than the state must control them with force. This restricts personal freedom.)

   e. ASK: Can you think of an illustration that supports that principle? Let them give several illustrations of their own. If they need help, you might suggest that they think of a situation of a child who obeys his parents. For example: If a child controls himself by obeying his parent's rule to not play in the street, then he has the freedom to play outside by himself. If he cannot control himself, then he must have someone watch him, or be confined to play inside a fenced yard, which limits his freedom.

2. DISCUSS the following quote by James Madison:

   "We have staked the whole future of the American civilization, not upon the power of government, far from it. We have staked the future. . . upon the capacity of each and all of us to govern ourselves, to control ourselves, to sustain ourselves according to the Ten Commandments of God." [2]

   a. ASK: Would our nation be a better, safer place if more people knew and tried to follow the Ten Commandments? (Yes) Have students elaborate why. What is it about the Ten Commandments that is helpful to society? If students do not mention it, draw out the significance of the fact that the Commandments are given by God, and that we must answer to Him for our behavior!

   b. ASK: In 1980 the Supreme Court ruled that the Ten Commandments could not be posted on the wall in public schools. Do you agree with that ruling? Why or why not? Help students give specific reasons by asking them follow-up questions to vague answers they may give. Ask questions like: Why do you say that? What biblical

principle would help you draw that conclusion? Play "devil's advocate" by taking the opposite position. Draw the more quiet students into the conversation. Lead them to see the connection between each of the worldview categories, i.e. how politics is based on law, which is needed to have an orderly society founded on ethical standards, that are needed because of our understanding of psychology, which comes from our biology as a result of our understanding of philosophy and theology! This is true for not only a biblical worldview, but for every other worldview (Humanism, Marxism, New Age, whatever) All these categories together make up one's "religious" view of life. Everybody's approach to life is "religious" in nature.

    c.   SUMMARIZE: SAY: **Teaching the Ten Commandments in school is not unconstitutional, since the primary author of the Constitution, James Madison, said what he did. Teaching about the Ten Commandments is not forcing "religion" on anyone; it is simply training children in the moral and legal basis for our society. For our nation to continue to be a country of freedom and opportunity, citizens need to know the principles which make our society and government work. As we learned two weeks ago, our laws are based on biblical principles. It is not coercing children to worship God when they are taught the moral principles that undergird a free society and the origins of those principles in the Bible. It is simply good education!**

3.   A PENNY FOR YOUR THOUGHTS: Give everyone a penny and ask them to read the two phrases on the side with the head of Lincoln. DISCUSS the following: **What is the connection between "Liberty" and "In God We Trust"? Can we have liberty apart from God? Why or why not?** Follow up this discussion with de Tocqueville's quote.

    Alexis de Tocqueville (1805-1859), in the 1830's was commissioned by the French government to travel throughout the United States in order to discover the secret of the astounding success of this experiment in democracy. The French were puzzled at the conditions of unparalleled freedom and social tranquility that prevailed in America. In fact, nowhere on earth was there so little social discord. Tocqueville reported:

    "Religion in America...must be regarded as the foremost of the politic institutions of that country; for if it does not impart a taste for freedom, it facilitates the use of it. I do not know whether all Americans have a sincere faith in their religion-for who can know the human heart?-but I am certain that they hold it to be indispensable for the maintenance of republican institutions... {America} is the place where the Christian religion has kept the greatest power over men's souls; and nothing better demonstrates how useful and natural it is to man, since the country where it now has the widest sway is both the most enlightened and the freest." [3]

4.   WORLDVIEW PERSPECTIVE: Ask students why they think so much time was spent on quoting the founding fathers during their daily assignments and this review. Help them understand that the ideas of the founders are timeless principles because they have their source in the Bible. Truth does not change over time. This relates to every worldview category we have studied so far. Trace the origin of the founders' thoughts through each of the worldview categories as it relates to their understanding of POLITICS. The following summaries will get you started. There is more that could be elaborated for each worldview category:

    THEOLOGY: God is the source of Justice, Liberty, and Morals which the state should uphold.

PHILOSOPHY: The Bible is true and we can know the truth. Politicians should seek out this truth and apply it to society.

BIOLOGY: We are created in God's image; therefore, the state should protect the worth of every person.

PSYCHOLOGY: We have fallen into sin; therefore, there is a need for "checks and balances" in government.

ETHICS: There is an objective moral code. The state should encourage all its citizens to live according to these moral principles. This will make it easier for the state to govern.

SOCIOLOGY: Society is comprised of several separate parts. The state is just one part of society and should not interfere with the domain of the family and church.

LAW: The basis for all law is the absolute ethical principles found in the Bible. Legislators should seek to "move" God's moral law into the realm of civil law.

5. MY WORLDVIEW HANDOUT: Give each student a handout, "My Christian Worldview of Politics," and have them guess which words go in the blanks. Help them fill in the blanks in the following manner: "My Christian worldview of politics states that government is **ordained** by God to protect the **innocent** from the evildoer. The only sound system of government is a system based on **biblical** principles. The Word of God recognizes both man's **sin** nature and man's rights based on his creation in the **image** and likeness of God. Even our branches of government: - the **legislative**, the **executive**, and the **judicial** - were derived from a **scriptural** model (Isaiah 33:22). In Matthew 22:15-22, Jesus explains that I must live in two kingdoms: the kingdom of **God** and the kingdom of **this world**. Therefore, I have a responsibility to see that **Godly** men and women are elected to public office in America. This is my **political** obligation as a follower of Jesus Christ."

6) TRANSITION: Now that we have reviewed politics, we will turn our attention to our next topic. To do that, we'll use our imaginations.

PART TWO: NEW TOPIC: ECONOMICS

I. INTRODUCTION

A. SCIENCE PROJECT PAYS OFF!: (If you are leading a college group, change the setting to reflect a campus scene.) Let's say that you do a science project on different kinds of dish detergent. During the experiment, you by accident mix two ingredients together that produce a dish detergent that makes baked-on lasagna fly off the pan, yet keeps your mom's hands as smooth as silk! In other words, you've just made a discovery of a new kind of dish soap! Since this is so revolutionary, you win first place in the regional, state, and national science project competition. Companies are calling you day and night asking to patent this new whiz-bang combination. You land a million dollar deal with Proctor and Gamble! And you haven't even gotten out of the 9th (make this appropriate to your class) grade!

1. ASK: What would you do with all of that money? (Various answers.)

2. ASK: Would having all that money make you happy? (Various answers.)

3. TRANSITION: **We sometimes think that having a lot of money would be the solution to all of our problems. But that's not always the case.**

B. REZNOR QUOTE: **Trent Reznor, lead singer of Nine Inch Nails and producer of Marilyn Manson, was** *Raygun's* **featured artist in February, 1997. At 31 years old, he not only sings but also produces millions of albums. Is he a happy and contented man? What do you think?** (Various answers.)

1. READ: Have students listen carefully as you read the following quote: **In the article, he said, "I'm also willing to acknowledge that I have changed as a result of my success . . . [but] I'm probably more sad right now than I've ever been, because I have the added baggage of . . . this [fame & money, which] didn't fix [my pain]. . . . I'm on a . . . path to self-destruction."**

2. ASK: **What can you conclude from Reznor's comments about money and happiness?** (Money does not make you happy.)

3. SUMMARY: **So having a lot of money does not guarantee being happy. But even though money does not bring happiness, we still have to have money to live.**

C. SHOP 'TIL YOU DROP: **Let's bring it back to reality, here in good ol' (<u>your town</u>). You did <u>not</u> win the national science competition, and you have <u>not</u> signed a million dollar deal. Instead, you are looking in your closet realizing that you have "nothing" to wear! You remember seeing a great $30 shirt and $40 pair of jeans at (The Gap, American Eagle, you name it) that you've been dying for.**

1. ASK SEVERAL STUDENTS: **How are you going to pay for that shirt and jeans? What if you didn't have enough money and you really wanted that outfit THIS WEEK!? What would you do?** (Various answers.)

2. SAY: **These are some really interesting questions about how we get what we want. When we ask these types of questions, we are discussing which of the 10 worldview categories?** (Economics) **I know that the word "economics" sounds dull and boring, but this deals with some things that are very real and pertinent to how you live your life every day. Let's face it, you can't live without money, right? So the question is, how do we get money and how should we spend money? These are the questions that "economics" deals with.**

3. SUMMARY: **This week, we are going to explore the world of money. How should we make it, how should we spend it, and who should be responsible for how it all works?**

4. TRANSITION: **In order to help us understand how the economy works, let's perform a short melodrama. You can help me.**

II. WHAT IS ECONOMICS?

A. "SWEET BETSY" MELODRAMA: Read the instructions for the "Sweet Betsy" melodrama found at the end of this lesson. When everyone has been assigned their parts, READ THE DRAMA.

 1. ASK: **What is the point of this little drama?** (It shows have the economy works; how people trade something they have for something they want. It also demonstrates the "division of labor," where people specialize in doing one thing that they trade for the other necessities of life.)

 2. DISCUSS: **How does this relate to our economy today? What is similar and what is different?** (Similar: division of labor. Different: We usually don't "barter." We work for money, then exchange money for food, clothing, etc.) **The addition of money makes the whole process run more smoothly and conveniently. We don't have to drive our herd of cattle down to The Gap to barter for a pair of jeans! It's a lot easier to take money; it's more portable!**

 3. TRANSITION: **This drama raises an interesting issue. That is, how do we get what we want? This is the basic question of economics. We'll take a closer look at that question next.**

B. GETTING WHAT WE WANT: **Basically, there are only two peaceful ways to get what you want in life.** NOTE: You may want to write the major ideas on the board as students respond. See words in CAPS below in #1, #2, and a. (1), a. (2), and a. (3).

 1. PRODUCE IT YOURSELF: **What would you say is one way to get what you want or need in life?** (Produce it or make it yourself.) **Right, like in the drama, Sweet Betsy's** (Pause to see if the group says their sound!) **daddy raised cows** (pause) **so he had all the beef** (pause) **he and his family could eat. That's one way to get what we need.**

 2. GET IT FROM OTHERS: ASK: **But what's another way?** (Get what we need from others who have it.) **Right again. Back to our drama. Cousin Ted made shoes,** (you may pause to keep "milking" the audience, or just keep going at this point. You know your group!) **so Sweet Betsy was able to get the shoes she needed from Ted.**

  a. THREE WAYS TO GET IT FROM OTHERS: **Now, there are actually three ways that you can get something from someone else. Let's see if you can come up with those three ways.** (As they guess correctly, write the following BOLD words on the board and elaborate as suggested)

   (1) GIFT: **Someone could give you what you wanted or needed with no strings attached - like if cousin Ted had decided to give Sweet Betsy shoes for her birthday.**

   (2) VOLUNTARY EXCHANGE: **This is what happened in the drama. Cousin Ted traded shoes for beef. It was voluntary. No one was forced to do it against his will. It was mutually beneficial to both Ted and Betsy.**

(3) THEFT: **This is taking what you want against the will of the person who has it. For example, Cousin Ted could have stolen some cows.**

3. SAY: **There is a reason that we have laws against theft. Do you know why?** (The Bible says, "Do not steal.") **This command in the Bible has some very important implications in regard to what our economy should look like. Actually, this is a starting point for our biblical worldview of economics.**

C. ECONOMIC "STEW": **But before we jump into the Bible, think with me for a minute about beef stew--you know, the kind your grandmother makes by cooking it on the stove for several hours as the aroma fills the house. A pot of stew has several ingredients. It may have potatoes, carrots, tomatoes, and beef. These ingredients blend together to give the stew its special flavor. If one of the ingredients is missing, it just doesn't taste the same. Well, the same thing is true when it comes to economics. There are several ingredients that go into what we might call an economic "stew." Each ingredient is important to giving the overall system a special flavor. And just like your grandmother's homemade stew, if we follow the biblical recipe, the economy will be good to everyone who tastes it, even down to the very bottom of the economic ladder!**

D. TRANSITION: **So let's find out what goes into a tasty economy. The Bible gives us some great ideas we can stir together.**

III. BIBLICAL PRINCIPLES OF ECONOMICS

A. TWO ECONOMIC SYSTEMS: Distribute the handouts, **"Shoes, Cows, and Economic Stew"** as you SAY: **First of all, we need to understand that there are basically two different systems of economics.** Have students refer to their handouts as you review the following:

1. **"SOCIALISM": In this system the government controls the means to produce and distribute goods. Communist countries operate under a socialist system of economics. In a purely socialist state, the government owns everything and is in charge of the factories, the farms, where people work, how much they make and how much things cost.**

2. **"FREE MARKET": In a "free market" economy, individuals are free to work where they want and use their material resources in the production of more wealth. The government plays only a small role, if any, in controlling what is produced, where people work and for how much.**

3. ASK: **These are two different ways people have organized their economies. Which system is used in our country?** (Allow some discussion. Use examples to help students understand that our nation was founded on "free market" principles, but over the last 50 - 60 years the government has taken over more and more control through taxes and regulation. This should not become a major debate at this point. Just let them see that these ideas are related to our situation here in the U. S.)

4. TRANSITION: **Our task today is to determine which is the better economic system according to the principles found in the Bible. Now the Bible does not give a detailed account of a system of economics, but it does give valuable principles concerning how to make and handle money. Once you know these principles, then you will understand how this fits into our total worldview.**

B. RESPONSIBILITY: Divide the class into three groups as you SAY: **The first part of the recipe for a biblical economic stew calls for a combination of things simmered together. Let's divide into three groups to search out what these are. In each group, look up the assigned verses, write a brief statement for each passage, and then try to summarize all the passages into one statement. After 6 minutes each group will share what they wrote with the rest of the class.** The following are suggested summaries. Your groups may come up with different summary statements.

   1. Group 1: <u>Work for $</u>
      a. Proverbs 10:4-5 - don't be lazy, but work
      b. Proverbs 24:33-34 - don't be lazy
      c. Proverbs 28:19 - don't chase fantasies

   2. Group 2: <u>Help others</u>
      a. Proverbs 22:9 - generous man is blessed
      b. Proverbs 28:27 - give to poor
      c. Ephesians 4:28 - work, share

   3. Group 3: <u>Be content</u>
      a. Philippians 4:12-13 - be content with what you have
      b. Hebrews 13:5 - don't love $ but be content
      c. 1 Timothy 6:10 - love of money is evil

   4. SUMMARY: **The emphasis of these verses is that we need to take responsibility to provide for ourselves and our families; then with the money we have made, we should share with those who have a need. And finally, we should be content with what we have and not make money our "god." To put all of these ideas into one category, you could use the word "responsibility." Write the word "responsibility" in the blank after ingredient #1. This summarizes the principles that we are responsible to work, responsible to care for others, and responsible to trust God.**

   5. TRANSITION: **But "responsibility" is only one ingredient for this recipe for economic "stew." There are a couple of other biblical principles that will help us understand how God has designed our economy to work the best.**

C. PERSONAL LIBERTY: **Let's look at the verses on your handout, Acts 5:1-4.** Read the passage aloud and SAY: **For our study today, we are not so concerned with the fact that this couple lied, but we want to look for a principle concerning how they handled their property.**

1. ASK: **What is revealed in Peter's statement about Ananias's ability to keep or sell his land? In other words, what is the underlying assumption behind Peter's statement?** (Ananias had control of his own property and the ability to do as he wished with it, i.e. to either keep it or sell it.) **How does this relate to the principle of socialism?** (This is basic to the concept of private property, or private ownership, in contrast to a socialist system of government ownership of all property.)

2. DO NOT STEAL: **This principle of Acts 5, the idea of ownership of private property, is also seen in the commandment against stealing. The command assumes that you have the rightful ownership of something. In this command not to steal, God established the idea of private ownership. As I mentioned earlier, this concept of private property is basic to all biblical principles of economics.**

3. SUMMARY: **So the principle here, that you can write as ingredient #2, is "freedom." The Bible indicates that each individual has the freedom to own things, to peacefully buy things, and sell things.**

4. WORLD SCOPE: **This is the type of freedom that we enjoy here in the United States. Did you know that only about one third of the world's population enjoys this same freedom? Two thirds of the people around the world are under the influence of a socialist system, where the government controls the businesses and means of making money.**

5. WORLDVIEW PERSPECTIVE: NASH QUOTE: **Look on your handouts to the quote by Ronald Nash: "Economic freedom aids the existence and development of political liberty by helping to check the concentration of too much power in the hand of too few people."**

   a. ASK: **According to this statement, what is the connection between economics and politics?** (Economic freedom, as in a free market economic system, acts as a check on political power, by distributing the wealth to many people instead of concentrating wealth in the hands of a few.)

   b. SIN NATURE: **We learned a valuable lesson a few weeks ago about the reason our founders provided a system of checks and balances in our government. Why was that?** (because of man's basic sin nature) **So our understanding of psychology, man's sin, not only helps us understand the role of politics, as in our government, but also our system of economics.**

   c. GOD'S IMAGE: **Our study of psychology helped us to understand two things about mankind. The first, as we just mentioned, is our sin problem. What is the second thing that makes up our basic nature?** (We are made in God's image.) **This tells us that we are individually important to God. That is why God holds us individually responsible, the first major principle we just looked at. And that is why we have the right to individual freedom. Remember what the *Declaration of Independence* said about our individual rights?** (We have a God-given, unalienable right, to life, LIBERTY, and the pursuit of happiness.) **That right to liberty means the freedom to choose your work (how you make money), and the freedom to own property**

thinking like a christian

(how you keep the money you make) and sell it as you please (how you spend money).

    d. SUMMARY: **The best economic system would take into account mankind's basic nature for greed and corruption, and would therefore not allow a few people to control the means of making money (socialism) for fear that those in power might use that power for their own selfish interest and limit the freedom of the people under their rule. On the other hand, God has designed us uniquely for individual freedom, and therefore holds us responsible for the work that we do. Do you see how these ideas are interconnected to form a total picture of a biblical worldview?** (pause for response) **Any questions so far?** (Respond to any questions at this point.)

D. JUSTICE: **A third ingredient in our economic stew has to do with "Justice." Write the word "justice" in the blank beside #3. This idea is found in Leviticus 19:15.** Read the verse and ASK: **Is God on the side of the poor as opposed to the rich? Why or why not?** (No, because that would not be just.)

    1. READ the anonymous quote on your handout and SAY: **Because people have different talents and use their talents in different ways, they will have different economic incomes. Under a socialistic system, the government tries to make everyone have the same amount. Is it just to take money from those who have more and give it to those who have less?** NOTE: There may be some discussion on this question. Allow some debate, asking for biblical reasons for their ideas. The following is a suggested answer to the question: No, it is not just. Because of the biblical principle just read, we must deal with all people the same. Although "life is not fair," and some people have more advantages than others, it is not just for the government to take away from one person (the wealthy) to give to another person (the poor). Jesus even said, "The poor you will always have with you." (Matthew 26:11.)

        NOTE: The passage in Acts 4:34-35 concerning those in the early church having all things in common does not relate to the government taking from some through taxes or other means, and giving the money to others. This was a unique situation in the early church and was done on a **voluntary** basis. The family and the church should help the poor, not the state.

    2. WORLDVIEW: ECONOMICS AND THEOLOGY: **Where does the idea of "justice" come from?** (From the very nature of God.) **God is just; it is a part of His Righteousness. So now we have connected economics with Theology! Again, the worldview picture fits together perfectly!**

    3. SUMMARY: **So the biblical worldview includes this idea of "justice" to mean that everyone should be dealt with justly, even though the results may be different. There will be some people who will be rich and some people who will be poor. This is a part of a total picture of the biblical view of economics. Families and the church should help those who are truly needy. It is the role of the state to maintain order and freedom, not redistribute the wealth of its citizens.**

E. TRANSITION: **Now that we've cooked up an economic stew from ingredients found in the Bible, let's try it and see how it tastes.**

IV. APPLICATION

    A. THE BIBLE, MONEY, AND YOU: On your handouts, there are listed two biblical principles that will help us apply what we've been discussing today.

        1. BE NEIGHBORLY: The first principle is "Be neighborly." Jesus said that we should treat our neighbors as we want to be treated, and He told the story of the good Samaritan to illustrate His point (Luke 10:25-37). Take a minute to take inventory of your life by answering the question on the handout: "Are you being neighborly with your money?" Allow a few minutes for individual reflection and writing.

        2. BE CONTENT: Another principle found in the Bible is the idea of contentment. The Apostle Paul said that he had learned to be content with what he had, whether it was a lot of money or barely enough to get by (Phil. 4:12-13). How do you feel about the amount of money you have or the things you own? Do you need to thank God for what He has provided for you? Do you need to ask Him for a feeling of contentment with what you have? Take a few minutes to reflect on that and write out a short prayer to God concerning your feelings about money.

    C. GRANDPARENT TALK: Sometime this week, ask your GRANDparents about what it was like growing up. Did they have a lot of money? Did they have to work for what they had? What are their views on our system of economics? After that, ask them the same questions about their parents, your great-grandparents! Then, share with them some of the principles you have learned today in class. Boy, will they be impressed with your great wisdom and learning!

    B. NEXT WEEK: Don't forget to continue your search for the world of ideas. Bring them with you next week. It will be our next to the last week in this worldview series. And be sure to spend time reviewing what you learned today by completing each day in your **JOURNAL**.

    C. CLOSE IN PRAYER.

Endnotes:
1) Quoted in *The Family Under Siege,* George Grant, Bethany House Publishers, 1994, p.175.
2) William J. Federer, *America's God and Country Encyclopedia of Quotations,* (Fame Publishing, Coppell, TX, 1994), p. 411.
3) Ibid., p. 204.

"sweet betsy" MELODRAMA

Instructions: Divide the class into the following groups and assign the sounds associated with each word in the story. Have each group practice their sound as you assign it to them. Instruct each group to make their sound every time their word is used in the story. Have at least 3 or 4 students in each group. If your class is small (fewer than 15 members) assign groups more than one sound or action.

Sweet Betsy = Cooooo   Shoes = Stomp their feet on the floor 4 times
Ranch/er = Yea-haw   Cowboy = Yeah-hoooo
Cow(s) or beef = Mooooo

Out in a remote west Texas **ranch** there lived a beautiful girl named **Sweet Betsy**. Now **Sweet Betsy** helped her daddy on the **ranch** by looking after the **cows**. One day **Sweet Betsy** was walking through the pasture and happened to step on a pile of **cow** stuff. Now the problem was that **Sweet Betsy** was not wearing **shoes**. As you can imagine, she was not very happy to have stepped in the **cow** stuff wearing no **shoes**. **Sweet Betsy** ran home to her daddy crying. She told him, "Daddy, I can stand it no longer. I must have some **shoes,** or else I refuse to tend the **cows** on our **ranch.**" Her daddy replied, "My dear, **Sweet Betsy**. I am but a **rancher**. All I know how to do is to raise **cows**. I do not have the time or the talent to make any **shoes.**"

Overhearing their conversation, a handsome **cowboy** named Ned happened by. He said, "Don't be in distress my good **rancher** and lovely maiden. I am a handsome **cowboy** named Ned with a cousin named Ted who makes **shoes**. My cousin named Ted is extremely fond of fresh **beef**. I, **cowboy** Ned, could ask Ted if he would exchange a pair of **shoes** for a side of **beef**. Wha'cha think?"

"Oh, **cowboy** Ned," said **Sweet Betsy**, "I'm sure ma daddy would be happy to trade **beef** for **shoes**. Would you, could you, **cowboy** Ned, ask your cousin Ted for a pair of little ol' **shoes** in exchange for some little ol' **beef**?"

"Y, certainly, **Sweet Betsy**, my dear." said **cowboy** Ned. "I'd be most honored." And so Ned did, and Ted did, and **Sweet Betsy** lived happily ever after wearing her new **shoes** as she tended the **cows** on her daddy's **ranch.** And everybody said TOGETHER (EVERYONE make your sound!).

John Jay

(1745-1829) was Governor of the state of New York, president of the American Bible Society (1821) and appointed by George Washington as the first Chief Justice of the Supreme Court. He said. . .

"No human society has ever been able to maintain both order and freedom, both cohesiveness and liberty apart from the moral precepts of the Christian Religion allied and accepted by all the classes. Should our Republic ere forget this fundamental precept of governance, men are certain to shed their responsibilities for licentiousness and this great experiment will surely be doomed."

Quoted in *The Family Under Siege,* George Grant, Bethany House Publishers, 1994, p.175.

thinking like a christian

James Madison

(1751-1836), known as the chief architect of the U.S. Constitution, was a member of the United States Congress where he introduced the Bill of Rights and was elected in 1809 as our 4th President. He said. . .

"We have staked the whole future of the American civilization, not upon the power of government, far from it. We have staked the future. . . upon the capacity of each and all of us to govern ourselves, to control ourselves, to sustain ourselves according to the Ten Commandments of God."

William J. Federer, *America's God and Country Encyclopedia of Quotations,*
(Fame Publishing Coppell, TX, 1994), p. 411.

John Adams

(1735-1826) our 2nd President, wrote. . .

"The Ten Commandments and the Sermon on the Mount contain my Religion. I agree perfectly with you [Thomas Jefferson], that 'The Moral Sense is as much a part of our Constitution as that of Feeling,' and in all that You say, upon this Subject."

The Adams-Jefferson Letters, (The University of North Carolina Press, 1987), p. 494.

Alexis de Tocqueville

(1805-1859), in the 1830's was commissioned by the French government to travel throughout the United States in order to discover the secret of the astounding success of this experiment in democracy. The French were puzzled at the conditions of unparalleled freedom and social tranquility that prevailed in America. In fact, nowhere on earth was there so little social discord. Tocqueville reported:

"Religion in America...must be regarded as the foremost of the political institutions of that country; for if it does not impart a taste for freedom, it facilitates the use of it. I do not know whether all Americans have a sincere faith in their religion-for who can know the human heart?-but I am certain that they hold it to be indispensable for the maintenance of republican institutions... {America} is the place where the Christian religion has kept the greatest power over men's souls; and nothing better demonstrates how useful and natural it is to man, since the country where it now has the widest sway is both the most enlightened and the freest."

William J. Federer, *America's God and Country Encyclopedia of Quotations,* (Fame Publishing Coppell, TX, 1994), p. 411.

thinking like a christian

shoes, cows, and economic stew

There are basically two systems of economics:

1. **"SOCIALISM":** the government controls the means to produce and distribute goods.

2. **"_____ MARKET":** individuals are free to use their material wealth (property, money, ideas) in the production of more wealth.

A BIBLICAL PERSPECTIVE ON MONEY
A Recipe for "Economic Stew"

INGREDIENT #1: _____

Group 1: _____

   Proverbs 10:4-5 -

   Proverbs 24:33-34 -

   Proverbs 28:19 -

Group 2: _____

   Proverbs 22:9 -

   Proverbs 28:27 -

   Ephesians 4:28 -

Group 3: _____

   Philippians 4:12-13 -

   Hebrews 13:5 -

   1 Timothy 6:10 -

INGREDIENT #2: _____

Acts 5:1-4

   1 Now a man named Ananias, together with his wife Sapphira, also sold a piece of property. 2 With his wife's full knowledge he kept back part of the money for himself, but brought the rest and put it at the apostles' feet. 3   Then Peter said, "Ananias, how is it that Satan has so filled your heart that you have lied to the Holy Spirit and have kept for yourself some of the money you received for the land? 4   Didn't it belong to you before it was sold? And after it was sold, wasn't the money at your disposal? What made you think of doing such a thing? You have not lied to men but to God."

Ronald Nash: "Economic freedom aids the existence and development of political liberty by helping to check the concentration of too much power in the hand of too few people."

INGREDIENT #3: _____

Leviticus 19:15 - "Do not pervert justice; do not show partiality to the poor or favoritism to the great, but judge your neighbor fairly."

> "Man is unequal in time allocated for him; talent entrusted to him; and treasure
>   required of him. Man is only equal to man before the bar of justice."
> - Anonymous (Quoted in *Understanding the Times,* p. 702)

THE BIBLE, MONEY, AND YOU!

1----> **Luke 10:25-37:** Are you being neighborly with your money?

2----> **Philippians 4:12-13:** Are you content with the things you have? Write a short prayer to God concerning your feelings about what you have or don't have:

GRANDPARENT TALK! This week, ask your grandparents what it was like for them growing up. Did they have a lot of money? Did they have to work for what they had? What is their view about our economic system? Then ask them the same questions about their parents to see how they might answer.

thinking like a christian

My Christian

WORLDVIEW

of politics

My Christian worldview of politics states that government is _____ by God to protect the

_____ from the evildoer. The only sound system of government is a system based on

_____ principles. The Word of God recognizes both man's_____nature and man's

rights based on his creation in the_____ and likeness of God. Even our branches of government,

the_____ ,the_____ , and the _____ , were derived from a

_____model. (Isaiah 33:22) In Matthew 22:15-22, Jesus explains that I must live in two

kingdoms, the kingdom of _____, and the kingdom of _____ _____. Therefore, I have a

responsibility to see that_____men and women are elected for public office in America. This is my

_____obligation as a follower of Jesus.

notes & ideas

overview
lesson 11

history: what about the past?

Don't ever think that history is boring. A biblical worldview of history brings all of the dull events of the past into multicolor focus. No longer is history just names and places and dates. From a worldview perspective there is purpose and direction to the flow of history. And more importantly, you learn the lessons of life that demonstrate God is there. History is truly HIS story.

Biblical history is "linear." It has a beginning ("In the beginning. . ." Genesis 1:1), a middle (we're in the middle now), and an end ("Then I saw a new heaven and a new earth. . ." Revelation 21:1).

Not only does history have a direction, it is a story. The story begins with God's relationship with the first man and woman, continues in his relationship with an entire nation (Israel), and concludes with his committment to the whole human race. But the pivotal point of the story is found in the life, death, and resurrection of Jesus, God's Son. What an awesome story!

His story gives meaning and purpose to our existence. It reveals that we are special to God. It shows us our destiny. And everything that happens is a part of His story. The Roman civilization with its system of roads, the middle ages with its monasteries, the Reformation with its religious leaders, the discovery of a "new world," the expansion of secular ideas during the late 1800's, and even the last presidential election: all is part and parcel of God's ultimate story of His involvement in human history.

This week as you teach the lesson on history, give students a vision of how the "world of ideas" puts flesh on the dry bones of historical events. Understanding God's perspective brings fresh life to the study of history, and it is an important part of understanding the times!

WOODROW WILSON, our 28th President, reminds us of the need to study the history of our nation. He said: "A nation which does not remember what it was yesterday, does not know what it is today, nor what it is trying to do. We are trying to do a futile thing if we do not know where we came from or what we have been about." (Quoted in *America's God and Country Encyclopedia of Quotations*, p.697.)

---

thinking like a christian

key concept: Jesus is the Logos made flesh.

key verse: 1 Timothy 3:16:

"Beyond all question, the mystery of godliness is great: He appeared in a body, was vindicated by the Spirit, was seen by angels, was preached among the nations, was believed on in the world, was taken up in glory."

objectives: By the end of this session, students should be able to

FOR THE REVIEW SESSION: ECONOMICS

. . . be convinced of the need for a free market economy.

. . . know the difference between "socialism" and "capitalism."

FOR NEW TOPIC: HISTORY

. . . relate how Christianity is a historical religion.

. . . chart the flow of history from God's perspective.

. . . commit themselves to being involved in the outworking of God's kingdom plan on earth.

read: U.T.T., Chapter 42, Biblical Christian History.

before class:

FOR THE REVIEW SESSION: ECONOMICS

☐ Provide a pencil and 3X5 card for each student.

☐ Make a copy of **"My Christian Worldview of Economics"** for each student.

☐ Purchase four "cool" pencils as prizes.

FOR NEW TOPIC: HISTORY

☐ Cut apart the different people and event squares from the **"Bible People and Events"** sheet, mix the order, and place in a box to be used during the lesson. NOTE: Read over the "Bible Time Line" section in the lesson to see the two ways to handle this activity. Depending on which alternative you choose, you may need some additional props.

☐ Make a copy for each student of the handout, **"History: Past, Present and Future."**

☐ Have a pencil for each student.

PART ONE: REVIEW ECONOMICS

1. CURRENT EVENTS: As students come into class, interact with them about current economic events in the news and how they relate to a biblical worldview.

2. PENCIL PARTS: Hold up a wooden pencil as you ASK: **What are the different parts of a pencil?** (Wood, graphite lead, metal, rubber, paint, lacquer.) As they respond, LIST ON THE BOARD the parts of a pencil.

   a. GROUPS OF 3-4: Divide class into groups of three or four, give to each group a 3 X 5 card and pencil as you SAY: **List as many different types of people and jobs that are required to produce a pencil in order that you are able to buy one in the store. Number each job or skill. Let's see which group can come up with the longest list in four minutes.**

      1) SHARE: Ask each group to share some of their ideas (not their whole list). After a few minutes, ask for the total number on their list. For the group that had the greatest number, give to each person in the group a new pencil as a prize.

      2) ASK: **Does any one government control the entire process of making a pencil?** (No.)

      3) ASK: **What do you think would happen if the government tried to control the process?** (If it could be done at all, pencils would be very expensive, in short supply, and not very well made!) **Why would this be the case?** (That is the nature of bureau-cracies.)

   b. SAY: **It's really incredible to think about all the people it takes just to make a thing like a simple pencil! But knowing what it takes to make a pencil raises some important questions for you and me concerning how we have any of the STUFF we enjoy in life - stuff like T.V.'s, V.C.R.'s, computers, cars, air-conditioned houses, toilet paper, and electric light bulbs.**

3. WORLDVIEW: **Thinking about all the stuff we have leads us to consider another of our worldview categories. As you've been studying this week, economics deals with more than just money. It answers what question?** (How should we gain and use material resources?)

   a. ASK: **What are the TWO SYSTEMS OF ECONOMICS?** Write the following on the board as they list each one:

      1) "SOCIALISM": Government controls the means of production.

      2) "FREE MARKET": Material wealth is used in the production of more wealth.

   b. ASK: **Which of the two systems fit better into the principles concerning money found in the Bible? Why?** Review the following principles:

      1) Work is a part of God's wonderful plan for our life. (Genesis 2:15)

      2) If you don't work, you don't eat. (2 Thessalonians 3:10)

thinking like a christian

3) Private property is key to freedom and prosperity. (Exodus 20:15 & 22:1-4)

4) We are stewards of God's resources. (Psalm 24:1)

4. SUMMARY PARAGRAPH: Give everyone the handout that summarizes their Christian worldview of Economics, and help them fill it in. It should read as follows: "My Christian worldview of Economics states that I believe in economic **responsibility,** economic **freedom,** and economic **justice.** According to the Bible, I am to **work** for my money [Proverbs 10:45], to **help** others [Proverbs 28:27], and to be **content** [Philippians 4:12-13]. In America, the ownership of **private** property is my God-given privilege, and in all my economic dealings I am to remember that I am only a **steward** of all, since all belongs to God."

5. REVIEW the "worldview perspective" on Day 4 in the **Student Journal** to show how all of this fits together to form a complete picture of life.

PART TWO: NEW TOPIC - HISTORY

I. INTRODUCTION

A. WORLDVIEW PUZZLE: Point to the "Worldview Puzzle" bulletin board as you SAY: **This week is a special time! Does anyone know what category we will be discussing today?** (History) **Right, history! How did you guess!? Oh, yea, it's the only one left on our worldview puzzle. Good thinking!**

1. ASK: **When you study history in school, does it ever seem boring?** (Various answers, but mostly "Yes, it's boring!".)

2. ASK: **Why is history boring?** (I don't see where it relates to my life. It's just a bunch of names, places, dates, etc.)

3. TRANSITION: **Well, today you will find out that history is anything but boring. In fact, like all of the other worldview categories, it relates to you in very specific ways. To find out about why history is important, think about this with me.**

B. THE MAN BORN YESTERDAY: Tell or read the story at the end of this lesson about the man born yesterday.

1. ASK: **What do these episodes from the movie tell you about the importance of history?** (We learn how to live our lives based on past experiences.) **The alien guy didn't know how to act because he had not learned about life; he was born only yesterday!**

2. ASK: **There are basically two ways to learn about life. What are they?** Allow students to respond, then summarize their answers with the following:

a. OUR EXPERIENCES: **We learn from OUR OWN EXPERIENCES. When the alien called the trucker "Jerk," he found out that was not a good thing to do.**

b. OTHERS' EXPERIENCES: **We learn from OTHER PEOPLE'S EXPERIENCES, like the alien learned to drive "very fast" when he saw the yellow light. He had learned that by watching the woman drive. This second way of learning is to learn from things that happened to other people in the past. We can do this by watching them or reading what they wrote. Either way, learning about life from other people's experiences is what we do when we study "history"!**

C. LEARNING FROM HISTORY: ASK: **Let me ask you another question. Why do little toddlers tend to walk out toward a busy street?** (They do not have the experience of life to know that cars might run over them.) **Because of their young age, they haven't learned from history, either from their own experience or from someone else's. That is why parents and older brothers and sisters instruct small children not to play in the street.**

1. WILSON QUOTE: Give each student a handout and pencil as you SAY: **Not only do we learn from the history of individuals, but we can learn principles of how to live based on the history of groups of people, or nations. Look on your handout at the quote by Woodrow Wilson, our 28th President. He reminds us of the need to study the history of our nation. He said: "A nation which does not remember what it was yesterday, does not know what it is today, nor what it is trying to do. We are trying to do a futile thing if we do not know where we came from or what we have been about."**

    a. ASK: **Why is it important to know where we came from as a nation?** (so we know what we should be doing today)

    b. WORLDVIEW CONNECTION: Have students relate Wilson's quote to our study of Law and Politics. This could be a short discussion about why it is important to learn about the religious ideas that are foundational to the way our political system was designed.

2. TRANSITION: **This illustrates some every important truths about why the study of history is crucial to your life and my life.**

D. HISTORY IS IMPORTANT: **How would you summarize what the study of history does for you today?** Summarize their answers under the following two headings:

1. IT SHOWS YOU WHAT <u>DOES NOT</u> WORK: **You learn not to walk out into a busy street or call a guy bigger than you "Jerk," because these things bring us pain!**

2. IT SHOWS YOU WHAT <u>DOES</u> WORK: **As we have been learning during this series, life goes better for us when we cooperate with the laws of nature, like the law of gravity, and the laws of God, like His moral laws. These laws show us how life is designed to work best. A good way to learn about these laws is through other people's experiences, or history. This shows us what we should do. For example, the Bible says to love others as you love yourself. This is a positive thing that we can put into practice. It is a practical principle that works for everyone! And we can see from other people's experience that life goes better when we practice the principle of love.**

E. TRANSITION: **So history is an important part of a worldview. It completes the picture for a total look at reality. Let's see what we can learn from history so that we don't have to make the same mistakes that other people have make in the past; and on the positive side, we can practice those things that make life work better.**

II. THE BIBLE AND HISTORY

A. AGREE/DISAGREE: SAY: **We will take a look at the Bible's view of history. As you think about the Bible, consider this statement:** *The Bible contains more history then it does philosophy and religion.* **Do you agree or disagree with that statement. I'll repeat it:** *The Bible contains more history than it does philosophy and religion.* **What do you think? If you agree, get up and stand over on the right side of the room. If you disagree, go stand over on the left side.** Allow students to move to either side.

1. ASK : **Why do you agree or disagree with the statement?** Allow discussion. Do not give them the "right" answer yet.

2. NOTE: If someone says that the Bible contains BOTH history and philosophy, say that you want them to make a choice. Remind them that this is an "agree/disagree" exercise, and repeat the statement. Prod their thinking, playing devil's advocate or pit one student's comment against another's.

3. SAY: **This has been a good discussion. In order to gain some perspective on this issue about the Bible and history, let's do a project together.**

B. BIBLE TIME LINE: Draw an imaginary "time line" on the floor in front of the class. Point out that one end represents the beginning of time and that it moves across the room to a time in the future. Explain that you have different people and events from the Bible written on pieces of paper and that you are going to have each student, one at time, pick a slip of paper from the can. Each student will read aloud what is printed on the paper, go to the imaginary "time line," place the piece of paper on the "line" where he thinks it should go, then return to his seat. Allow discussion among the group as to where a person or event should go. If you have fewer students than people/events, you can give some students a second turn until all of the people and events are placed.

ALTERNATIVE METHOD: Instead of drawing an imaginary line on the floor, tape a piece of string across the room or front wall. Have students clothespin the pieces of paper to the "clothesline" time line.

1. When all the events and people have been placed, SAY: **Now that we have our Bible time line, let's consider the statement I made a few minutes ago: "The Bible contains more history then it does philosophy and religion." How do you respond to that statement now?** (Allow discussion.)

2. SAY: **Actually, both philosophy and history are contained in the Bible. But the difference is this. God has communicated philosophical and religious ideas THROUGH the historical events told in the Bible, so the history that is told reveals to us how God works in the world.**

thinking like a christian

3. ASK students to mention historical events from the Bible that reveal religious ideas. Allow brief discussion as they share.

C. 1 CORINTHIANS 10 STUDY: SAY: **The apostle Paul said that the history of the Old Testament is written to teach us lessons about life. Turn in your Bibles to 1 Corinthians 10:1. Let's read several verses together. See if you can tell me what events Paul is describing in this passage.** Read **1 Corinthians 10:1-6**.

1. ASK: **What events in the nation of Israel is Paul describing?** (Moses is leading the nation of Israel out of the land of Egypt. "Under the cloud" refers to the pillar of cloud that guided the Israelites through the desert by day. The "sea" refers to the Red Sea, etc.)

2. ASK: **But all of this history, these events in the nation of Israel, Paul says happened for a purpose. What is that purpose?** (To teach us by being an example of what NOT to do, i.e., disobey God.)

D. SUMMARY: **The Bible gives us history and this history has a purpose. That purpose is to teach us Godly principles for living. But what is the story that is told in the Bible. Let's take a closer look at the history of the Bible.**

III. THE BIBLE AND HISTORY

A. BIBLE DISCOVERY: SAY: **Look again at our time line. What do you notice about the time frame that it represents?** (There is the past, the present, and the future.) Refer students to the handout. Have them work individually or in groups, or together in a large group, to look up the passages and discuss them. NOTE: The point of this exercise is to demonstrate that "history" has a flow, a direction. Do not get side-tracked onto specific issues during this discussion. Try to keep the focus on the "big picture" while still engaging students in relevant discussion. A few suggestions follow:

1. PAST:

    a. Genesis 1:1 - God began history. **When did "time" begin?** ("In the beginning") **Before the creation, there was no such thing as "time." God created matter, space, and time "in the beginning."**

    b. Romans 5:12 - Adam's fall affected all future generations, leading to hatred, envy, war, etc.

    (1) ASK: **Did Paul consider the story of Adam and Eve as myth or did he view them as real people who lived in the past?** (true historical people)

    (2) ASK: **If Adam and Eve were not real people, how would that affect biblical psychology?** (There would be no basis for the idea that mankind is basically sinful if this were just a made-up story. The whole biblical worldview would break down if what the Bible says is not true history!)

2. PRESENT:

    a. Romans 8:28 - God is in sovereign control of all things. **When things don't go the way you want them to go, can you still trust God for what happens?** (yes, because he is in control and He loves and cares for me)

    b. Genesis 50:19-20 - God can use even evil men for His purposes.

3. FUTURE:

    a. Revelation 20:11-15 - There will be a final judgment for all people. **How do you know that there will be a final judgment?** (Because God has been at work in the past and present, we can be assured that He will continue His work in the future!)

    b. Revelation 21:1-4 - There will be a new heaven and new earth and God will dwell among mankind. **How is this future event different from how we live in the present?** (no wars, disease, etc.) **Are you motivated to be a part of this "new earth"?**

4. SUMMARY: **We learn from this that history is "linear." In other words, it goes in a straight line. It has a beginning, a middle and an end. It is heading toward an ultimate purpose, and that purpose includes you!**

B. HISTORY IS "HIS STORY": SAY: **Someone has said that history is really "His story," meaning the story of Jesus Christ. Jesus was in the beginning with God; His first coming was foretold by the prophets, and He will sit as judge in the future, final judgement.**

1. ASK: **Apart from these roles, Jesus stands out as the centerpiece of history because of one thing. Do you know what that is?** (his death and resurrection)

2. 1 CORINTHIANS 15:3-8 STUDY: Have everyone turn to the passage and discuss the facts of the resurrection as an event in history. ASK probing questions such as:

    a. **Is the resurrection a myth or history? How do we know that Jesus actually rose from the dead?** (See Luke 24:1-3; John 20:1-8. The body of Jesus was no longer in the tomb.)

    b. **Were there any eyewitnesses to the resurrection? If so, who?** (Yes, see above passages: Mary, Mary Magdalene, Peter, John.)

    c. **Are the testimonies of the eyewitnesses reliable? Why or why not?** (Yes, because they died martyrs' deaths for what they knew to be true: the resurrection.)

3. 1 CORINTHIANS 15:14-19 STUDY: Look at these verses and discuss the significance of the historical resurrection of Jesus. ASK: **What difference would it make if Jesus had not been raised from the dead?** (Paul would be found to be a liar, the dead are not raised, we are still in our sins, and we are to be pitied for believing a lie!)

4. SUMMARY: **It must be pretty important to know for sure that the resurrection of Jesus did take place! Christianity stands or falls on this one issue: the resurrection of Jesus. If Jesus did not rise from the dead, then you are a fool to be a Christian. But because of the historical validity of the empty tomb and resurrection appearances of Jesus, we can be assured that our faith is based on historical facts. Our faith in Jesus is not a blind faith, but a faith based on the facts of an empty tomb and the resurrection appearances of Jesus!**

C. TRANSITION: **Because of what happened in the past, we have a solid foundation upon which to build our worldview. This knowledge about Jesus' resurrection gives us great assurance about our future relationship with God. Finally, the resurrection leads us to consider how we should live our lives in the present.**

IV. HOW THEN SHOULD WE LIVE?

A. APPLICATION: 2 PETER 3:10-14 - SAY: **Let's look at a New Testament passage that focuses on how we should live in the present.** Have students individually read the 2 Peter passage and write out a specific application of how they can live a holy and blameless life.

1. DISCUSS: After several minutes of reflection and writing, ask if anyone would share their thoughts with the class. Again, use this time to help them be specific in their application of God's Word. Gently probe them to consider what it means to their life in specific ways to be "holy" or "blameless."

   a. ASK: **Specifically, what does that mean you would do or not do with your family, with your friends, or with your peers?**

   b. ASK: **How does Bible study play a part in the process of "holy living"?**

   c. ASK: **Can you still have "fun" and live a holy life? Define what you mean by "fun." Look up "fun" in your Bible concordance. Guess what? The word is not there! Now look up the word "joy." What does that tell you about God's focus for your life? What's the difference between "fun" and "joy"?**

B. NEXT WEEK: **Next week we will wrap up our entire study on a biblical worldview.**

   1. ARTICLES: **Again, let me encourage you to look for articles in the paper, magazines, or assignments in class, and think about the worldview perspective that is being expressed. Bring them to our session next week.**

   2. JOURNALS: Remind everyone to complete their Journals during the week and bring them to the next session. If they have completed all of the assignments, they will be eligible for the special event that you have planned.

C. Close in prayer.

My Christian

WORLDVIEW

of Economics

My Christian worldview of economics states that I believe in economic _____, economic

_____, and economic _____. According to the Bible, I am to _____ for my money

[Proverbs 10:45], to _____ others [Proverbs 28:27], and to be _____ [Philippians 4:12-13]. In

America, the ownership of _____ property is my God-given privilege, and in all my economic

dealings I am to remember that I am only a _____ of all, since all belongs to God.

the man born yesterday

There was a movie that came out a few years ago about an alien life form that came to earth and floated about in the house of a young woman who had just recently lost her husband. It landed on a strand of hair from the woman's dead husband. The alien life united with the DNA in the hair and cloned itself into a fully-grown replica of the man who had died. This new "man" stayed up all night speed-reading the encyclopedia. He could absorb information very quickly, but still everything about human life on earth was new to him. He had to learn it for the first time.

As you can imagine, life became very interesting for him, especially when the wife woke up to find someone who looked just like her husband. Together, they had to drive across the country to meet the alien spaceship at a designated place in Arizona. Along the way, the woman had to teach the new alien everything about life.

At one point they had stopped to eat at a road-side truck stop. The alien had overheard some of the men talking, and one of them used the phrase, "You jerk!" As the two were leaving the cafe, the alien accidently bumped into a trucker. The alien looked straight at the trucker and said, "You jerk!" The trucker hauled off and hit the alien. The woman had to pull a gun to get the trucker to back off.

Later, the woman asked the alien to drive the car so she could sleep. The alien had been observing her drive and said that he could do it. As they were traveling down a long stretch of highway, they approached a stop-light that had turned to yellow. The alien started going faster. An 18-wheeler was coming from the side street and was pulling into the intersection. The alien pushed the gas peddle to the floor as their car sped toward the truck. Just before they reached the intersection, the light turned red and the alien slammed on the brakes, putting the car into a skid, just missing the truck. The woman yelled at the alien guy, saying, "I thought you knew how to drive! Don't you know what a yellow light means?!" The alien replied, "I watched you very carefully. Green means go. Red means stop. Yellow means go <u>very fast</u>!"

Bible people and events

Cut apart along dashed lines. Mix the order and place in a container.

creation	adam & eve	the flood
abraham	slavery in egypt	moses
promised land	the judges	samuel
king david	the exile	daniel
nehemiah	Jesus	peter
paul	white throne judgement	new heaven & new earth

thinking like a christian

history: past, present and future

history is important:

IT SHOWS YOU WHAT_____WORK:

IT SHOWS YOU WHAT_____WORK:

God works through history

past:

Genesis 1:1 -

Romans 5:12 -

present:

Romans 8:28 -

Genesis 50:19-20 -

future:

Revelation 20:11-15 -

Revelation 21:1-4 -

the centerpiece of history:
I Corinthians 15:3-8 & 14-19 -

how should we then live?
2 Peter 3:10-14 -

notes & ideas

lesson 12

conclusion: putting it all together!

This last lesson may be the most important one in the series for three reasons.

First, it gives you the opportunity to review the entire series. This review puts together the whole picture in a way that demonstrates the centrality of "theology" to the biblical worldview; what one thinks about God is the foundation for what one thinks about every other area of life. While we understand culture's problems are primarily theological in nature, we need to learn the art of presenting solutions in a way that will gain a hearing in an increasingly secular society. To do that involves a certain amount of "cross-cultural" communication. This study will help students see how to take a subject, such as psychology, and trace it back to its theological roots.

There is a second reason this lesson is strategic. We are in the midst of a "culture war." This culture war is, in reality, a battle over worldviews. There are three major worldviews that have aligned themselves against the Biblical Christian worldview: Secular Humanism, Cosmic Humanism (New Age), and Marxist-Leninism. These three worldviews are introduced at this point to alert students to the fact that there is a battle for their minds, and it is taking place all around them: in the media, especially in TV and the movies; in education, especially on the university campuses; and in our political system, especially on the federal level. To better understand these other worldviews, a second series of lessons is being written which contrasts the Biblical Christian view with Secular Humanism, Cosmic Humanism, and Marxist Leninism. Contact Summit Ministries for the availability of this next curriculum.

Third, this lesson will challenge studens to continued action. Based on several Scriptural passages, action points are developed as students think about how God might direct them to be a part of the solution to today's cultural problems. This curriculum only lays the groundwork of the biblical worldview. There is much more that needs to be learned. Hopefully, they will see the need for further study.

The best way to learn about the religious worldviews of our day is to attend a Summit Ministries "Leadership Conference." Contact Summit Ministries for more information concerning their summer student conferences or their adult conferences held in the winter and spring. You can reach Summit Ministries at PO Box 207, Manitou Springs, Co, 80829, (719) 685-9103, or visit their website at www.summit.org Their website has a wealth of information on each of the four worldviews as presented in this study and the text, *Understanding the Times*.

---

lesson twelve

conclusion

key concept: Jesus is the basis of a Christian worldview.

key verses: Colossians 2:6-8

"So then, just as you received Christ Jesus as Lord, continue to live in him, rooted and built up in him, strengthened in the faith as you were taught, and overflowing with thankfulness. See to it that no one takes you captive through hollow and deceptive philosophy, which depends on human tradition and the basic principles of this world rather than on Christ."

objectives: By the end of this lesson, students should be able to

    . . . demonstrate an appreciation for how the Bible gives a comprehensive "worldview."

    . . . present a plan of action based on their new knowledge.

    . . . summarize other worldviews (i.e. Secular Humanism, New Age, and Marxism).

    . . . see the need for further study in order to better "understand the times."

read: U.T.T., CONCLUSION, p. 367-402.

before class:

FOR THE REVIEW SESSION: HISTORY

☐ Make a copy for each student of the handout, **"My Worldview of History"** and have pencils available.

FOR NEW TOPIC: CONCLUSION

☐ Make a copy for each student of the handouts, **"The World of Worldviews"** and **"Culture Wars: What You Can Do."**

PART ONE: REVIEW HISTORY

NOTE: This review session is intentionally kept short in order to give more time to the Summary of the entire study and overview of competing worldviews.

1. ARTICLES: Review any articles that students brought.

2. SUMMARY PARAGRAPH: Help the students fill in their summary paragraph for history. It should read as follows: "My Christian worldview of history reflects the **Bible's** use of history to communicate God's **philosophical** and **religious** ideas to man. Truth is expressed through **history,** so the study of history teaches me **lessons** about life. God speaks about the past, the present, and the future; there fore I have a **linear** view of history. There is a **purpose** to all of history. The most significant historical event is the **resurrection.** I am called to live a **diligent** and **blameless** life until the day of the Lord."

PART TWO: NEW TOPIC - CONCLUSION

I. INTRODUCTION:

SAY: Educators tell us that repetition aids learning, so today, we are going to review all ten categories that make a worldview. Also, we are going to see that our biblical worldview is being attacked by other worldviews that are dominant in many areas of our society.

II. REVIEW ALL TEN CATEGORIES:

A. This review session can be led in TWO different ways.

1. OPTION A: Lead a group discussion where everyone participates freely.

2. OPTION B: Have some "friendly competition" by dividing the group into two or more "teams" and keeping score. Scoring can be as follows: Question #1 under each category = 5 points. Question #2 = 10 points. Question #3 = 12 points. Question #4 = 15 points. Suggested answers are in (...).

3. WORLDVIEW PUZZLE: In either case, refer to the articles taped to the bulletin board (collected over the duration of this study) as examples or illustrations as each category is discussed.

4. INTRODUCE the class to the option you have selected.

B. THEOLOGY: ASK the following questions:

1. We started our study with Theology, which asks what question? (What about God: Is there a God and what is God like?)

2. What is the biblical answer to that question? (God is Ruler, Relational and Righteous.)

3. So what? In other words, how does your understanding of this area relate to your life? (Since God is Righteous, I need to pay attention to what He says about life

and how I should live it! Since God is relational, He desires a relationship with me and sent Jesus to be the payment for my sin problem. Because God Rules, He can enforce His moral laws in the final judgment.)

C. PHILOSOPHY: ASK the following questions:

1. **What is the question?** (What about reality: What is real and how do I know?)

2. **What is the Biblical Christian answer?** (Reality consists of two parts: the natural universe and the supernatural realm.)

3. **How is the nature of God reflected in this area?** (God is supernatural, yet He created the natural universe. God has not left the universe to operate by itself, but He still plays a vital part in it.)

4. **So what?** (There is more to my life than just my physical body. I can experience eternal life because God is eternal.)

D. BIOLOGY: ASK the following questions:

1. **What is the question?** (What about life: what is the origin of life?)

2. **What is the Biblical Christian answer?** (God created life and designed living things to reproduce after their own kinds.)

3. **How is the nature of God reflected in this area?** (God is an eternal living Being; therefore He was able to impart "life" to plants and animals.)

4. **So what?** (I owe my life to God. I can see evidence of God's design in nature by studying His creation. Evolution, as a process of time + chance + matter, is scientifically impossible.)

E. PSYCHOLOGY: ASK the following questions:

1. **What is the question?** (What about mankind: what is man's basic nature?)

2. **What is the Biblical Christian answer?** (People are created in God's image, yet are sinful.)

3. **How is the nature of God reflected in this area?** (We are created in God's image; therefore, we reflect His characteristics of moral consciousness, and dominion over the other animals, and we desire relationships with God and other people. However because of our sin nature, we cannot have a relationship with God apart from His saving grace in Christ Jesus.)

4. **So what?** (I cannot experience a relationship with God unless my sins are forgiven through accepting Jesus' death for me.)

F. ETHICS: ASK the following questions:

1. **What is the question?** (What about morality: what is right and wrong behavior?)

2. **What is the Biblical Christian answer?** (There are moral absolutes that serve as objective standards by which to measure our behavior.)

thinking like a christian

3. **How is the nature of God reflected in this area?** (God's moral standards by which we are to live reflect His character of love, truth, holiness, forgiveness, grace, etc.)

4. **So what?** (Biblical ethics give me a set of ideals that I should strive to live by. They also show me that I am sinful and in need of a savior.)

G. SOCIOLOGY: ASK the following questions:

1. **What is the question?** (What about society: how should we live together in groups?)

2. **What is the Biblical Christian answer?** (There are three levels of society: the family, the church, and the state.)

3. **How is the nature of God reflected in this area?** (God is relational, and He created the family to satisfy our need for close relationships. God is truth, and He designed the church to guide us into spiritual truth. The state is designed to maintain order, because God is a God of order.)

4. **So what?** (We should allow each level of society the freedom to function according to God's design. I should work at building close relationships with my family, participate in the work and mission of the church, and obey the government where it does not conflict with God's commands.)

H. LAW: ASK the following questions:

1. **What is the question?** (What about laws: what are the rules that run the universe and human life?)

2. **What is the Biblical Christian answer?** (God designed certain principles, called "natural laws," into the fabric of the universe: the physical world, the moral realm, and the civil arena.)

3. **How is the nature of God reflected in this area?** (Laws reflect God's orderly nature. They demonstrate how God designed things to work properly.)

4. **So what?** (By studying God's world and God's Word, I can discover the laws that He designed into the "nature of things." This leads me to understand scientific laws, moral laws, and rules for civil government.)

I. POLITICS: ASK the following questions:

1. **What is the question?** (What about government: how should we be governed?)

2. **What is the Biblical Christian answer?** (Government should do two things: punish the person who does wrong and protect the one who does right.)

3. **How is the nature of God reflected in this area?** (God punishes sin and rewards those who live according to His laws.)

4. **So what?** (I have an unprecedented opportunity to be involved in the democratic process of my country and should exert a moral influence on our government.)

J. ECONOMICS: ASK the following questions:

1. **What is the question?** (What about money: how should it be made, and how should it be spent?)

2. **What is the Biblical Christian answer?** (Work is ordained by God and is the means by which we earn our food and shelter. People should be free to peacefully buy and sell goods and services.)

3. **How is the nature of God reflected in this area?** (God "worked" in creating the universe and man. We also work.)

4. **So what?** (Work is honorable and is a part of God's plan for mankind. I should use my God-given gifts in meaningful work, and then be willing to share with those in need.)

K. HISTORY: ASK the following questions:

1. **What is the question?** (What about the past"?)

2. **What is the Biblical Christian answer?** (History is linear; it had a beginning, a middle, and is headed toward an end. The future is bright for the Christian. But for those who reject Christ, there is eternal hell.)

3. **How is the nature of God reflected in this area?** (God rules over the events of history. Since God is righteous, He must judge our sin. Yet, because He desires a relationship with us, He sent Jesus as the centerpiece of history to redeem us. In the future, God, through Christ, will judge all people, who will then be assigned to either the new heaven and the new earth or to hell for eternity.)

4. **So what?** (I should be motivated to share with my friends and others about the life-giving love and forgiveness that Jesus offers. Because God is in control of history, I can learn from the past and do not have to fear the future.)

L. TRANSITION: **This review should be a constant reminder to each of us that our faith in God is not just a personal and private thing. The Christian religion involves a total way of looking at all of life. We have a consistent, biblical worldview.**

III. THE WORLD OF WORLDVIEWS

A. OTHER WORLDVIEWS: Give each student the handout, **"The World of Worldviews."**

1. READ the following quote by Dr. James Dobson and Gary Bauer: **"Nothing short of a great Civil War of Values rages today throughout North America. Two sides with vastly differing and incompatible worldviews are locked in a bitter conflict that permeates every level of society ...."** The war... is a **"struggle for the hearts and minds of people. It is a war over ideas."** (Quoted in *Understanding the Times,* p. 1)

thinking like a christian

2. SAY: **Did you realize that there are other worldviews vying for your attention? We have alluded to them during these past eleven weeks. Do you know what they are called?** (WRITE the following on the board as they are mentioned: Secular Humanism, New Age, Marxism. You may need to give the answers.)

B. SECULAR HUMANISM: SAY: **Take for example, Secular Humanism. This worldview is based on the ideas of philosophers dating back hundreds of years, but it was formalized in 1933 with the publication of "The Humanist Manifesto." This little booklet was signed by a number of very influential Americans, including John Dewey, the man considered to be the founder of modern public education. The manifesto was updated in 1973.**

1. ASK: **How have you been influenced by Secular Humanism?** (Since John Dewey was so influential in public education and he was a Secular Humanist, the humanist worldview must be evident in our educational system.)

2. BIOLOGY: **To understand how Humanism has influenced our education system, all you have to do is consider just one area of study, Biology. Let's review how the origin of life is taught in most Biology classes today and trace its worldview foundation.**

   a. ASK: **What is taught about the origin of life?** (It evolved by a mindless, purposeless process.)

   b. ASK: **As we saw during our study of Biology, evolution is based on what philosophy?** (Naturalism = nature is all there is to reality.)

   c. ASK: **And naturalism rests on what Theology?** (Atheism = no god)

   d. DISCUSS: **Secular Humanism starts with mankind (the "human" element) and sees everything as "secular" (there is nothing "sacred" = related to God). As atheists, they assume (without proof) that nature is all there is to reality (naturalism); therefore, the only option left open to them concerning the origin of life is the evolution of dead matter into living systems. Do you see how a religious worldview like Humanism is being presented as scientific fact in Biology classes?** Allow some discussion in order for the point to sink in. This is crucial for students to understand if they have not gotten it so far.

3. SO WHAT? SAY: **The "so what" is that Humanism is a total worldview and has something to say about each of the worldview categories on our board. It's easy to see that the Humanist worldview is the exact opposite of Biblical Christianity in each area. Humanist ideas are tearing at the fabric of our nation, trying to take it down a different path from the biblically based traditions on which it was founded. For that reason, you need to know what Humanists believe, who they are, and what their agenda is for our country.**

4. TRANSITION: **Humanism is only one worldview that is trying to draw you away from biblical ideas. There are others.**

thinking like a christian

187

C. MARXISM: SAY: **Marxism is a second worldview that is waging war with Christianity. It is named after Karl Marx who wrote the "Communist Manifesto" in 1848. His writings, along with those of Vladimir Lenin, form the basis of communism. Vast numbers of the world's population today live under communist control.**

1. ASK: **How are you influenced by Marxism?** Most students will probably say that they are not influenced by Marxism. READ to them the following:

   a. ARTICLE: **In an article titled "Marxism in U.S. Classrooms," U.S. News and World Report reported that there are ten thousand Marxist professors on America's [university] campuses. Georgie Anne Geyer says that "the percentage of Marxist faculty members can range from an estimated 90 percent in some midwestern universities."** (*Understanding the Times,* p. 5)

   b. QUOTE: **Dr. Fred Schwarz says, "The colleges and universities are the nurseries of communism."** (*Understanding the Times,* p. 6)

2. HISTORY: SAY: **Let's see how Marxists have had an influence in one area of study: history. Pretend that you are a Marxist history professor. As a good Marxist, you are an atheist. In fact, you recall that Lenin wrote, "Religion is opium for the people." As you know, opium is an illegal drug. ASK: Here in America what do we say about illegal drugs?** (Just say no!) **If religion is like a drug, then what do you say about religion?** (Just say no!)

   a. ASK: **Then as a Marxist history professor about to write a textbook for the school children across America, how do you treat religion in general and particularly Christianity?** (Leave out any references to how religion/Christianity has helped society, such as founding hospitals, etc. and include only negative examples such as the Crusades of the Middle Ages or the Salem witch trials in the 1600's. Do not give any examples of how religion played a vital role in the founding of America or is a current influence in our society.)

   b. ASK: **Do you realize this is exactly the case in history textbooks? Can you think of any positive examples of religion that you studied in your history class in high school?** (Allow time for discussion.) **What negative images of religion do you recall?** (The Crusades and Salem witch trials, plus others they may mention.)

   c. QUOTE: Read the following quote by Paul Vitz who surveyed the way religion and traditional values are represented in 90 widely used reading and social studies textbooks in public school. **"Religion, traditional family values, and conservative political and economic positions have been reliably excluded from children's textbooks."** Paul C. Vitz, *Censorship: Evidence of Bias in our Children's Textbooks* (Ann Arbor, Mich.: Servant, 1986.)

3. THE POINT: **Even if you don't feel the influence of Marxism today, you definitely will if you go to almost any college or university in America. And guess where all of our public school teachers are trained? Right, our colleges and universities. Many teachers are being influenced by Marxist ideas and then these ideas are transmitted to the elementary and high**

thinking like a christian

school classrooms, often by teachers who are not fully aware where these ideas originated. For that reason alone, you need to know something about the Marxist worldview.

IMPORTANT NOTE: We are not saying that all public school teachers are Secular Humanists or Marxists. There are many Christian teachers working in our public schools. Yet, even these Christian teachers are being taught by Secular Humanists and Marxist faculty on the university campus; and if these teachers are not aware of the leanings of their professors, they can be influenced to embrace some of the tenets of a Marxist worldview without realizing the significance of what they are being taught.

D. NEW AGE: SAY: **The New Age movement is also a comprehensive worldview. Some estimates put the the number of New Agers in America as high as 10 percent of the population. New Age is simply ancient Hindu religion dressed up in modern language. For example, back in the 60's, the Beatles traveled to India, embraced the Hindu religion, and began to write songs from a New Age perspective. These songs influenced a whole generation of young people who are now in their 40's and 50's, folks who are in positions of leadership throughout our community. New Agers believe that "everything is god," including the rocks, trees, dolphins, and you!**

   1. NEW AGE INFLUENCE: ASK: **How have New Age ideas influenced your life?** Allow some discussion. If students cannot come up with any examples, suggest the following: **Meditation is a central ingredient of New Age philosophy.**

      a. STAR WARS: The original Star Wars Trilogy: Luke Skywalker is taught to meditate by the little Jedi Master, Yoda, a prime example of an eastern guru!

      b. *PUMSY*, an elementary school curriculum which supposedly teaches "self-esteem", instructs children to meditate by visualizing an inner "friend." Biblically we would call it a "spirit guide", which is forbidden in Scripture.

   2. SAY: **Because of its widespread influence, you need to know something about the New Age worldview.**

E. TRANSITION: **What should be our response to these competing worldviews?**

IV. APPLICATION

A. CULTURE WARS: **Today, we reviewed the biblical worldview. But also, we introduced the fact that there are three other major worldviews that have significant influence in our country. Each of these worldviews is opposed to Biblical Christianity. That is why there is a "culture war" going on in our country.**

   1. ASK: **Where is the battleground for this culture war?** (In your mind.)

   2. ASK: **What are the weapons being used?** (The world of "ideas.")

   3. SAY: **These ideas may sound enticing and already have led many people away from the truth found in the Bible. The battle lines are drawn over**

abortion, gay rights, homosexual marriage, tolerance, "safe-sex" education, prayer in school, posting the Ten Commandments on a courtroom wall, public taxes going to support "gay" art, allowing pornography on the Internet, you name it!

B. WHAT YOU CAN DO: SAY: **It's not enough just to know about the culture war surrounding us. Like a good soldier, we must be willing and prepared to do something about it. On your handout are three passages that will help us zero in on what we can do to enter the war over ideas.** Have someone read 1 Peter 3:15-17 as everyone follows along on their handout.

1. BE PREPARED: **1 Peter 3:15-17** - "But in your hearts set apart Christ as Lord. Always be prepared to give an answer to everyone who asks you to give the reason for the hope that you have. But do this with gentleness and respect, keeping a clear conscience, so that those who speak maliciously against your good behavior in Christ may be ashamed of their slander. It is better, if it is God's will, to suffer for doing good than for doing evil."

    a. SAY: **There are tons of ideas in this passage that you can pick out to apply to your life. As you have learned throughout these lessons, be sure to make your application specific to your life. Don't write general comments like, "Read the Bible more." Get really specific about what it means to obey this portion of God's word. What are you going to do? When will you do it? Why is it important to do it? These questions will help you put into practice what God is leading you to do with your life. Take three minutes to write one or two things that stand out in your mind.**

    b. SHARE: After three minutes, ask for volunteers to share what they have written. NOTE: Do the same with the other two passages. Read the verse, have them write their action points, and then ask for several to share with the group what they wrote. You might want to suggest ways that the entire group can be involved in some action point, such as the entire group attending a City Council meeting to better understand local government and then come back to the next meeting with their ideas about the issues facing the city.

2. BE WISE: **Proverbs 21:22** - "A wise man attacks the city of the mighty and pulls down the strong hold in which they trust."

3. UNDERSTAND THE TIMES: That is why it is so important that you learn more so you can be like the man of Issachar in the Old Testament, who "understood the times" and "knew what they ought to do" (1 Chronicles 12:32).

C. CLOSE IN PRAYER: Form a circle, hold hands, and suggest that several students pray for God's wisdom in understanding the times and for accomplishing their action points.

final note to group leader

This ends the formal class instruction on a biblical worldview, but it is only the tip of the iceberg. This curriculum was the first step in a life-long journey in understanding "worldviews" and knowing what to do from a biblical perspective. Here are several suggestions for continuing the process of "understanding the times."

1) **be a leader:** Attend an adult Christian Leadership conference sponsored by Summit Ministries. For a brochure on adult conferences, write or call **Summit Ministries, PO Box 207, Manitou Springs, CO, 80829, (719) 685-9103,** www.summit.org. Summit Ministries equips tomorrow's servant leaders to understand worldview analysis and champion the Christian Worldview, inspiring them to love God with their hearts, souls, minds, and strength. For over 35 years, Summit Ministries has admonished Christians to avoid being captured by the wisdom of the world (Colossians 2:8), and encouraged them to take captive every thought for Christ (2 Corinthians 10:5).

2) **be a reader:** Set up a reading plan in order to better understand the issues confronting the church today. Call the **Summit Bookhouse, (719) 685-9103,** for a list of thoughtful worldview-oriented books available in the Christian community.

3) **be involved:** Pick one of the ten categories or current issue of the day that has special interest to you and determine to become more knowledgeable in that area. Read books and look for articles that deal with that area. Then seek out opportunities to engage the culture from a biblical perspective.

For example, if you are interested in the abortion issue, read three or four of the excellent books that deal with a Christian response to the arguments for "a woman's right to choose." Then, write thoughtful letters to the editor, or organize a group to picket an abortion clinic, or work at a "pro-life" counseling center in your town. If there is not a pro-life counseling center, network with people from the churches in your area to start one.

Whatever you choose, be sure to become informed on the issues and know the biblical responses. In that way, you will gain a hearing from the secular world and can use that hearing as a bridge to present the Gospel, which is the ultimate solution to the troubles in our society.

4) **be influential:** Seek to influence other Christians to develop a worldview perspective. Here are three suggestions:

A) **youth:** TEACH the Worldviews in Focus Part 2 curriculum dealing with Secular Humanism, Marxism, and New Age philosophies. Call Summit Ministries to order the material.

B) **adults:** HOST a Worldview Weekend event in your area. Call Summit for speakers and the names of other people who have organized these conferences for youth, college students and adults.

C) **teachers:** PUBLIC, PRIVATE, SUNDAY SCHOOL: INITIATE a worldview training session for school teachers in your area for which they receive CEU credit. Summit Ministries has information packets that you can give to your local school administration with the details for this kind of training. Also, training is available for Sunday school teachers to present their weekly lessons from a worldview perspective.

We pray for God's blessings as you seek to serve Him by "understanding the times" and "knowing what to do."

Because He lives,
David Noebel and Chuck Edwards

thinking like a christian

My Christian

wor{dview

of History

My Christian worldview of history reflects the _____ use of history to communicate God's _____

and _____ ideas to man. Truth is expressed through _____, so the study of history teaches

me _____ about life. God speaks about the past, the present, and the future; therefore I have a

_____ view of history. There is a _____ to all of history. The most significant historical event

is the _____. I am called to live a _____ and_____ life until the day of the Lord.

the world of worldviews

"Nothing short of a great Civil War of Values rages today throughout North America. Two sides with vastly differing and incompatible worldviews are locked in a bitter conflict that permeates every level of society. The war is a struggle for the hearts and minds of people. It is a war over ideas."
(Quoting Dr. James Dobson and Gary Bauer in *Understanding the Times,* p.1)

three religious worldviews of our day:

1. **secular** _____: Based on the Humanist Manifestos of 1933 and 1973, this worldview starts with mankind and sees everything as "secular" (there is no "sacred" = God). As atheists, secular humanists assume that nature is all there is to reality (_____).

    How are you influenced by Secular Humanism?

    Teaching Biology in a secular age:

2. **marxism** is named after Karl Marx who wrote the Communist Manifesto (1848). This atheistic worldview is similar in many ways to Secular Humanism.

    How are you influenced by Marxism?

    The "university connection":

    Teaching history:

3. **new age:** Take ancient Hindu religion, dress it up with modern overtones, and you come up with the notion that "everything is god."

    How have New Age ideas influenced your life?

    _____ is a central ingredient of New Age philosophy.

culture wars: what you can do

BE PREPARED:

"But in your hearts set apart Christ as Lord. Always be prepared to give an answer to everyone who asks you to give the reason for the hope that you have. But do this with gentleness and respect, keeping a clear conscience, so that those who speak maliciously against your good behavior in Christ may be ashamed of their slander. It is better, if it is God's will, to suffer for doing good than for doing evil." 1 Peter 3:15-17

ACTION POINT:

BE WISE:

"A wise man attacks the city of the mighty and pulls down the stronghold in which they trust." Proverbs 21:22

ACTION POINT:

UNDERSTAND THE TIMES:

You should be like the men of Issachar, who "understood the times and knew what Israel should do..." 1 Chronicles 12:32

ACTION POINT:

For more information about worldviews and how you can influence others for Jesus Christ, contact **Summit Ministries, PO Box 207, Manitou Springs, Co 80829, (719) 685-9103.** www.summit.org

thinking like a christian

Leader's Guide to the Fact Sheets

In this section, we've provided you with Fact Sheets on a variety of topics, complete with key quotes and sources for more information. Our hope is that these fact sheets will become a good basis for helping students think about the cultural, moral and theological issues of our day.

As You Use These Fact Sheets, Keep a Few Things in Mind:

■*These Fact Sheets are Just a Start.* We've begun the research work, but haven't done it all for you! Hopefully, these quotes and sources will get you started, but none of the lists are meant to be comprehensive – there's always more good stuff out there!

■*Finding the Other Good Stuff.* When you've looked up the books on these lists, turn to the back and look at the bibliography and end notes to find out who the author is using for information. Then, look up those books! Write to the organizations listed and ask them for more information; talk to people who know about your subject and ask for references. Each source should lead you to other sources.

■*Getting Great Quotes.* Your most powerful quotes will come from people who shouldn't be saying what they are saying. (This is particularly important when you're writing for a non-Christian instructor.) For example, a quote by an evolutionist saying the fossil record doesn't support evolution is more powerful than a similar quote from a creationist.

■*Credibility.* Make sure the people you quote and the sources you use have the greatest credibility possible. Go to original sources whenever possible – don't simply quote Christian authors talking about what other people think.

■*Use Discretion.* Don't assume that an author is a Christian just because we have them on our Fact Sheets, or that Summit Ministries would agree with everything that person has said or written. In some cases, we've quoted sources that we definitely disagree with so you can see what another viewpoint is saying.

Abortion

UNDERSTANDING THE TIMES

Key Quotes

"Many people are very, very concerned with children in India, with the children of Africa where quite a few die of hunger, and so on. Many people are also concerned about all the violence in this great country of the United States. These concerns are very good. But often these same people are not concerned with the millions who are being killed by the deliberate decision of their own mothers. And this is what is the greatest destroyer of peace today – abortion, which brings people to such blindness."

Mother Teresa, quoted in Cal Thomas, "Meek Mother Teresa delivers a verbal knockout punch,"
Colorado Springs Gazette Telegraph, 9 February 1994, B7.

"'The nurses have to look at the ultrasound picture to gauge how far along the baby is for an abortion, because the larger the pregnancy, the more you get paid. It was very important for us to do that. But the turnover definitely got greater when we started using ultrasound. We lost two nurses – they couldn't take looking at it. Some of the other staff left also.' What about the women having the abortions? Do they see the ultrasound? 'They are never allowed to look at the ultrasound because we knew that if they so much as heard the heartbeat, they wouldn't want to have the abortion.'"

Dr. Joseph Randall, who performed over 32,000 abortions, quoted in David Kupelian and Mark Masters,
"Pro-Choice 1991: skeletons in the closet," *New Dimensions*, September/October 1991, 43.

"The fact that restricting access to abortion has tragic side effects does not, in itself, show that the restrictions are unjustified, since murder is wrong regardless of the consequences of prohibiting it; and the appeal to the right to control one's body, which is generally construed as a property right, is at best a rather feeble argument for the permissibility of abortion. Mere ownership does not give me the right to kill innocent people whom I find on my property, and indeed I am apt to be held responsible if such people injure themselves while on my property. It is equally unclear that I have any moral right to expel an innocent person from my property when I know that doing so will result in his death."

Prochoice philosopher Mary Anne Warren, "On the Moral and Legal Status on Abortion," in *The Problem of Abortion*,
2d ed., ed. Joel Feinberg (Belmont, CA: Wadsworth, 1984), p. 103, quoted in Randy Alcorn,
Pro Life Answers to Pro Choice Arguments, (Portland, OR: Multnomah Press, 1992), p. 86.

"A nurse who had worked in an abortion clinic for less than a year said her most troubling moments came not in the procedure room but afterwards. Many times, she said, women who had just had abortions would lie in the recovery room and cry, 'I've just killed my baby. I've just killed my baby.'

"'I don't know what to say to these women,' the nurse told the group. 'Part of me thinks "Maybe they're right."'" Diane M. Gianelli, "Abortion providers share inner conflicts," American Medical News, 12 July 1993, 36.

SUMMIT MINISTRIES

FACT SHEET

Summit Ministries
does not necessarily endorse all the views and
ideas represented by these sources.

PO BOX 207
MANITOU SPRINGS, CO 80829
(719) 685-9103

Key Sources

Alcorn, Randy. *Pro-Life Answers to Pro-Choice Arguments*. Portland, OR: Multnomah, 1992.
    This is the KEY book on this topic, pulling together resources from many others. Also includes extensive appendixes of organizations and pro-life resources.
Ankerberg, John, and John Weldon. *When Does Life Begin?* Brentwood, TN: Wolgemuth and Hyatt, 1989.
Beckwith, Francis J. *Politically Correct Death: Answering Arguments for Abortion Rights*. Grand Rapids, MI: Baker Books, 1993.

Gianelli, Diane M. "Abortion providers share inner conflicts." American Medical News, 12 July 1993, pp. 3, 36-37.

Grant, George. Grand Illusions: The Legacy of Planned Parenthood. 2nd ed. Franklin, TN: Adroit Press, 1988, 1992.

Kasun, Jaqueline. The War Against Population: The Economics and Ideology of Population Control. San Francisco, CA: Ignatius Press, 1988.

Key Organizations

National Right to Life
419 Seventh St., Suite 402
Washington, D.C. 20004

Christian Action Council
701 W. Broad St., Suite 405
Falls Church, VA 22046

WEBA (Women Exploited By Abortion)
Route 1, Box 821
Venus, TX 76084
(214) 366-3600

Key Verses

Genesis 1:27
Exodus 20:13; 21:22,23
Psalm 139:13-16
Proverbs 24:11,12
Jeremiah 1:5

Creation

UNDERSTANDING THE TIMES

Key Quotes

"The essential point of creation has nothing to do with the timing or the mechanism the Creator chose to employ, but with the element of design or purpose. In the broadest sense, a 'creationist' is simply a person who believes that the world (and especially mankind) was *designed*, and exists for a *purpose*."
Phillip E. Johnson, *Darwin on Trial*, (Downers Grove, IL: Inter Varsity Press, 1991), p. 113.

"Science is possible only because we live in an ordered universe which complies with simple mathematical laws. The job of the scientist is to study, catalogue and relate the orderliness in nature, not to question its origin. But theologians have long argued that the order in the physical world is evidence for God. If this is true, then science and religion acquire a common purpose in revealing God's work."
Paul Davies, *God and the New Physics*, (New York: Simon and Schuster, 1983), p. 144.

"[A]t this moment it seems as though science will never be able to raise the curtain on the mystery of creation. For the scientist who has lived by his faith in the power of reason, the story ends like a bad dream. He has scaled the mountains of ignorance; he is about to conquer the highest peak; as he pulls himself over the final rock, he is greeted by a band of theologians who have been sitting there for centuries."
Robert Jastrow, *God and the Astronomers*, (New York: W.W. Norton, 1978), p. 116.

"A science which deals with origin events does not fall within the category of empirical science, which deals with observed regularities in the present. Rather, it is more like a forensic science, which concentrates on unobserved singularities in the past. That is, a science about origins is a singularity science about the past; it differs from a scientific understanding about singularities in the present. A science about the past does not observe the past singularity but must depend on the principle of uniformity (analogy), as historical geology and archaeology do."
"Just as a forensic scientist tries to make a plausible reconstruction of an unobserved (and unrepeatable) murder, so the evolutionist and creationist attempt to construct a plausible scenario of the unobserved past singularities of origin. So neither view is operation science. Rather, both are in the domain of origin science."
"Some events of origin may have nonnatural primary intelligent causes. But to insist on finding a natural cause where there is evidence for primary intelligent causes is like demanding that a geology class remain at Mount Rushmore until it discovers some natural process of erosion to explain the faces formed on the mountainside."
Norman L. Geisler and J. Kerby Anderson, *Origin Science: A Proposal for the Creation-Evolution Controversy*, (Grand Rapids, MI: Baker Book House, 1987), pp. 14, 25, 30.

Key Verses

Genesis 1:1
Genesis 1:27
Mark 10:6
John 1:1-3
Colossians 1:16,17
Hebrews 11:3

SUMMIT MINISTRIES

FACT SHEET

Summit Ministries
does not necessarily endorse all the views and
ideas represented by these sources.

PO BOX 207
MANITOU SPRINGS, CO 80829
(719) 685-9103

Key Sources

Bauman, Michael, ed. *Man and Creation: Perspectives on Science and Theology.* Hillsdale, MI: Hillsdale College Press, 1993.

Geisler, Norman L., and J. Kerby Anderson. *Origin Science: A Proposal for the Creation-Evolution Controversy.* Grand Rapids, MI: Baker Book House, 1987.

Johnson, Phillip E. *Darwin on Trial.* Washington, DC: Regnery Gateway, 1991.

Lester, Lane P., and Raymond G. Bohlin. *The Natural Limits To Biological Change.* 2nd ed. Dallas, TX: Probe Books/Word Books, 1989.

Moreland, J. P., ed. *The Creation Hypothesis: Scientific Evidence for an Intelligent Designer.* Downers Grove, IL: Inter Varsity Press, 1994.

Taylor, Paul S. *Origins Answer Book.* Mesa, AZ: Eden Productions, 1991.

Key Organizations and Publications

Origins Research, a quarterly published by Students for Origins Research, PO Box 38069, Colorado Springs, CO 80937-8069.

Institute for Creation Research, 10946 Woodside Ave. N., Santee, CA 92071.

Key Creationists

Kurt P. Wise
Hugh Ross
Duane Gish
John Morris
Henry Morris
Charles Thaxton

Reliability of Scripture
UNDERSTANDING THE TIMES

Key Quotes

"The earliest preachers of the gospel knew the value of...first-hand testimony, and appealed to it time and again. 'We are witnesses of these things,' was their constant and confident assertion. And it can have been by no means so easy as some writers think to invent words and deeds of Jesus in those early years, when so many of His disciples were about, who could remember what had and had not happened....

"And it was not only friendly eyewitnesses that the early preachers had to reckon with; there were others less well disposed who were also conversant with the main facts of the ministry and death of Jesus. The disciples could not afford to risk inaccuracies (not to speak of willful manipulation of the facts), which would at once be exposed by those who would be only too glad to do so. On the contrary, one of the strong points in the original apostolic preaching is the confident appeal to the knowledge of the hearers; they not only said, 'We are witnesses of these things,' but also, 'As you yourselves also know' [Acts 2:22]. Had there been any tendency to depart from the facts in any material respect, the possible presence of hostile witnesses in the audience would have served as a further corrective."

> F. F. Bruce, *The New Testament Documents: Are They Reliable?*, 5th ed.
> (Downers Grove, IL: Inter Varsity Press, 1960), pp. 45-46.

"There is no body of ancient literature in the world which enjoys such a wealth of good textual attestation as the New Testament."

> F. F. Bruce, *The Books and the Parchments*, Rev. ed., (Westwood: Fleming H. Revell, 1963) p. 178.

"There is, I imagine, no body of literature in the world that has been exposed to the stringent analytical study that the four gospels have sustained for the past 200 years. This is not something to be regretted: it is something to be accepted with satisfaction. Scholars today who treat the gospels as credible historical documents do so in the full light of this analytical study, not by closing their minds to it."

> F. F. Bruce, "Foreword," in *The Historical Reliability of the Gospels*,
> Craig Blomberg, (Downers Grove, IL: Inter Varsity Press, 1987) p. ix.

"Skepticism toward the reliability of Scripture seems to survive in many academic circles despite the repeated collapse of critical theories. One still finds a disposition to trust secular writers whose credentials in providing historical testimony are often less adequate than those of the biblical writers. Not long ago many scholars rejected the historicity of the patriarchal accounts, denied that writing existed in Moses' day, and ascribed the Gospels and Epistles to second-century writers. But higher criticism has sustained some spectacular and even stunning reverses, mainly through the findings of archaeology. No longer is it held that the glories of King Solomon's era are literary fabrication, that 'Yahweh,' the redemptive God of the Hebrews, was unknown before the eighth-century prophets, or that Ezra's representations about the Babylonian captivity are fictional. Archaeologists have located the long-lost copper mines of Solomon's time. Tablets discovered at Ebla near Aleppo confirm that names similar to those of the patriarchs were common among people who lived in Ebla shortly before the events recorded in the later chapters of Genesis took place."

> Carl F. H. Henry, "The Authority of the Bible," in *The Origin of the Bible*,
> Philip Wesley Comfort, ed., (Wheaton, IL: Tyndale House, 1992) p. 17.

SUMMIT MINISTRIES

FACT SHEET

Summit Ministries
does not necessarily endorse all the views and
ideas represented by these sources.

PO BOX 207
MANITOU SPRINGS, CO 80829
(719) 685-9103

Key Verses

Psalm 14:1; 199:89
Isaiah 40:8
Matthew 5:18; 24:35
Mark 13:31
Luke 1:1-4; 16:17; 21:33
Acts 1:1-3; 2:32

1 Corinthians 15:1-9
2 Timothy 3:16
Hebrews 11:6
2 Peter 1:16
1 John 1:1-3
Revelation 22:18-19

Key Sources

Archer, Gleason L. *Survey of Old Testament Introduction.* Rev. ed. Chicago, IL: Moody, 1994.

Blomberg, Craig. *The Reliability of the Gospels.* Downers Grove, IL: Inter Varsity Press, 1987.

Bruce, F. F. *Are the New Testament Documents Reliable?* 5th ed. Downers Grove, IL: Inter Varsity Press, 1960.

_____. *The Canon of Scripture.* Downers Grove, IL: Inter Varsity Press, 1988.

Carson, D. A., and John D. Woodbridge, eds. *Scripture and Truth.* Grand Rapids, MI: Zondervan, 1983.

_____. *Hermeneutics, Authority and Canon.* Grand Rapids, MI: Zondervan, 1986.

Comfort, Philip Wesley, ed. *The Origin of the Bible.* Wheaton, IL: Tyndale House Publishers, 1992.

Free, Joseph P. *Archaeology and Bible History.* Rev. ed. Grand Rapids, MI: Zondervan, 1992.

Geisler, Norman L., ed. *Inerrancy.* Grand Rapids, MI: Zondervan, 1980.

Geisler, Norman L., and William E. Nix. *A General Introduction to the Bible.* Rev. ed. Chicago, IL: Moody Press, 1968, 1986.

McDowell, Josh. *Evidence That Demands A Verdict.* 2 vols. San Bernardino, CA: Here's Life, (1972) 1979, (1975) 1981.

Thompson, J. A. *The Bible and Archaeology.* Grand Rapids, MI: Eerdmans, 1989.

Warfield, Benjamin B. *The Inspiration and Authority of the Bible.* Phillipsburg, NJ: Presbyterian and Reformed Publishing, 1948. (This is the classic on the inspiration, authority and inerrancy of the Bible.)

Key Players

Gleason L. Archer, *Trinity Evangelical Divinity School, Deerfield, IL*
Craig Blomberg, *Denver Seminary, Denver, CO*
F. F. Bruce, (deceased)
D. A. Carson, *Trinity Evangelical Divinity School, Deerfield, IL*
Norman L. Geisler, *Southern Evangelical Seminary, Charlotte, NC*
Walter C. Kaiser, Jr., *Trinity Evangelical Divinity School, Deerfield, IL*
J. I. Packer, *Regent College, B. C., Canada*
Moises Silva, *Westminster Seminary, Philadelphia, PA*
Benjamin B. Warfield, (deceased)

Moral Relativism
UNDERSTANDING THE TIMES

Key Quotes

"There is one thing a professor can be absolutely certain of: almost every student entering the university believes, or says he believes, that truth is relative. If this belief is put to the test, one can count on the students' reaction: They will be uncomprehending. That anyone would regard the proposition as not self-evident astonishes them, as though he were calling into question 2 + 2 = 4.... Openness—and the relativism that makes it the only plausible stance in the face of various claims to truth and various ways of life and kinds of human beings—is the great insight of our times.... The study of history and of culture [according to this view] teaches that all the world was mad in the past; men always thought they were right, and that led to wars, persecutions, slavery, xenophobia, racism, and chauvinism. The point is not to correct the mistakes and really be right; rather it is not to think you are right at all.

"The students, of course, cannot defend their opinion. It is something with which they have been indoctrinated."

Allan Bloom, *The Closing of the American Mind*, (New York: Simon and Schuster, 1987) pp. 25-26.

"The fundamental question of ethics is, who makes the rules? God or men? The theistic answer is that God makes them. The humanist answer is that men make them. This distinction between theism and humanism is the fundamental division in moral theory."

Max Hocutt, "Toward an Ethic of Mutual Accommodation," in *Humanist Ethics*, ed. Morris B. Storer (Buffalo: Prometheus Books, 1980), p. 137.

"No inherent moral or ethical laws exist, nor are there absolute guiding principles for human society. The universe cares nothing for us and we have no ultimate meaning in life."

William Provine, "Scientists, Face It! Science and Religion are Incompatible," *The Scientist*, 5 September 1988, 10.

" . . . we can rationally discuss and argue with each other about right and wrong without resorting to the claim that ethical judgments are merely subjective or relative and that all such judgments have equal validity. For to claim the latter logically leads one to the bizarre judgment that Mother Teresa is no more and no less virtuous than Adolf Hitler."

Frank Beckwith, "Philosophical Problems With Moral Relativism," *Christian Research Journal*, Fall 1993, 39.

"If there is no absolute beyond man's ideas, then there is no final appeal to judge between individuals and groups whose moral judgments conflict. We are merely left with conflicting opinions."

Francis A. Schaeffer, *How Should We Then Live?* (Old Tappan, NJ: Fleming H. Revell, 1976), p. 145.

Key Verses

Exodus 20
Psalm 12:8
Proverbs 14:12; 16:25
Isaiah 5:20-23
Amos 5:15
Matthew 7:13
Romans 1:18-32; 12:9
Hebrews 5:14

SUMMIT MINISTRIES

FACT SHEET

Summit Ministries
does not necessarily endorse all the views and
ideas represented by these sources.

PO BOX 207
MANITOU SPRINGS, CO 80829
(719) 685-9103

Key Sources

Bennett, William J., ed. *The Book of Virtues: A Treasury of Great Moral Stories.* New York: Simon and Schuster, 1993.

Beckwith, Francis J., and Michael E. Bauman, eds. *Are You Politically Correct?: Debating America's Cultural Standards.* Buffalo, NY: Prometheus Books, 1993.

Bloom, Alan. *The Closing of the American Mind.* New York: Simon and Schuster, 1987.

Burke, Thomas J., ed. *The Christian Vision: Man and Morality.* Hillsdale, MI: The Hillsdale College Press, 1986.

Davis, John Jefferson. *Evangelical Ethics: Issues Facing the Church Today.* 2nd ed. Phillipsburg, NJ: Presbyterian and Reformed Publishing, 1985, 1993.

Hunter, James Davison. *Culture Wars: The Struggle to Define America.* New York: Basic Books, 1991.

Kilpatrick, William. *Why Johnny Can't Tell Right from Wrong: Moral Illiteracy and the Case for Character Education.* New York: Simon and Schuster, 1992.

Sowell, Thomas. *Inside American Education: The Decline, the Deception, the Dogmas.* New York: The Free Press, 1993.

Sykes, Charles J. *A Nation of Victims: The Decay of the American Character.* New York: St. Martin's Press, 1992.

Key Advocates of Relativism

Joseph Fletcher, *Situation Ethics*, deceased
Paul Kurtz, President, American Humanist Association
Lester Kirkendall, *A New Bill of Sexual Rights and Responsibilities*
Corliss Lamont, *The Philosophy of Humanism*

Feminism
UNDERSTANDING THE TIMES

Key Quotes

"The Christian worldview is intimately familiar with the experience of emptiness, with the despair and impotence that radical feminists – like all of us – seek to escape. We call this experience the human condition. Christians know the dark night of the soul, but we also know that self-glorifying rage will only plunge us deeper into the abyss."   Katherine Kersten, "How the Feminist Establishment Hurts Women," *Christianity Today*, June 20, 1994, 25.

"...the only thing so ubiquitous in the feminist's field of vision that she finds it everywhere she looks is herself."   Michael Levin, *Feminism and Freedom*, (New Brunswick, NJ: Transaction Books, 1988), p. 300.

"There can't be a relationship where two people are working to make changes in the world. Something has to give. Someone has to be focused on the kids. I think Arnold has made some changes in his life, but one of us had to be flexible enough to be there for our kids all the time." (Maria Shriver articulating what many women have found about "trying to do it all.")
Marilyn Beck, "Maria Shriver Changes Priorities," *Colorado Springs Gazette Telegraph TV Guide*, July 10-16, 1994, 4.

"Feminists are becoming difficult to identify, not because they do not exist, but because their philosophy has been integrated into mainstream society so thoroughly. The philosophy is almost unidentifiable as *feminist*, for it is virtually indistinguishable from *mainstream*."
Mary A. Kassian, *The Feminist Gospel*, (Westchester, IL: Crossway Books, 1922), p. 251.

"I have taught feminist theory. I have debated gender feminists on college campuses around the country, and on national television and radio. My experience with academic feminism and my immersion in the ever-growing gender feminist literature have served to deepen my conviction that the majority of women's studies classes and other classes that teach a 'reconceptualized' subject matter are unscholarly, intolerant of dissent, and full of gimmicks. In other words, they are a waste of time."
Christina Hoff Sommers, *Who Stole Feminism?: How Women Have Betrayed Women*, (New York: Simon & Schuster, 1994), p. 90.

Key Sources

*Blotnick, Srully. *Otherwise Engaged: The Private Lives of Successful Career Women*. New York: Facts on File Publications, 1985. (Reports results of a 25 year study of the professional and private lives of over 2,000 women.)
Kassian, Mary. *The Feminist Gospel*. Westchester, IL: Crossway Books, 1992.
*Farrell, Warren. *The Myth of Male Power*. Simon & Schuster, New York, 1993.
Gilder, George. *Men and Marriage*. Gretna, LA: Pelican, 1986.
*Levin, Michael. *Feminism and Freedom*. New Brunswick, NJ: Transaction Books, 1988.
Mitchell, Brian. *Weak Link: The Feminization of the American Military*. Washington, DC: Regnery-Gateway, 1989.
*Sommers, Cristina Hoff. *Who Stole Feminism? How Women Have Betrayed Women*. New York: Simon & Schuster, 1994.
Piper, John, and Wayne Grudem, eds. *Recovering Biblical Manhood and Womanhood*. Wheaton, IL: Crossway Books, 1991.
See also: "Key Sources" on *Marriage and Family* Fact Sheet.

*These books are not written from a Christian perspective, (and may contain false premises) but will provide some good sources for refuting the ideas of feminism.

Key Verses

Ephesians 2:3, 1 Corinthians 11:10,11, Galatians 3:28, 1 Peter 3:4, Proverbs 31:30

SUMMIT MINISTRIES

FACT SHEET

Summit Ministries does not necessarily endorse all the views and ideas represented by these sources.

PO BOX 207
MANITOU SPRINGS, CO 80829
(719) 685-9103

America's Godly Heritage
UNDERSTANDING THE TIMES

Key Quotes

"... Having undertaken for the Glory of God, and the Advancement of the Christian Faith, and the Honour of our King and Country, a Voyage to plant the first colony in the northern Parts of Virginia; Do by these Presents, solemnly and mutually in the Presence of God and one another, covenant and combine ourselves together into a civil Body Politick...."

The Mayflower Compact, Nov. 11, 1620, reprinted in Documents of American History,
ed. Henry Steele Commager, 9th ed. (Englewood Cliffs, NJ: Prentice-Hall, 1973), pp. 15-16.

"The general principles, on which the Fathers achieved independence, were ... the general principles of Christianity."

John Adams, in a letter to Thomas Jefferson, June 28, 1813, reprinted in The Adams-Jefferson Letters,
ed. Lester J. Cappon (Chapel Hill, NC: University of North Carolina Press, 1959), vol. 2, pp. 339-40.

"There is no country in the whole world, in which the Christian religion retains greater influence over the souls of men than in America: and there can be no greater proof of its utility, and of its conformity to human nature, than that its influence is most powerfully felt over the most enlightened and free nation of the earth. [1835]"

Alexis de Tocqueville, Democracy in America (New Rochelle, NY: Arlington House, n.d.), vol. 1, p. 294.

"Of all the dispositions and habits which lead to political prosperity, Religion and morality are indispensable supports. In vain would that man claim the tribute of Patriotism, who should labour to subvert these great Pillars of human happiness, these firmest props of the duties of Men and citizens.... And let us with caution indulge the supposition, that morality can be maintained without religion. Whatever may be conceded to the influence of refined education on minds of peculiar structure, reason and experience both forbid us to expect that National morality can prevail in exclusion of religious principle.

"'Tis substantially true, that virtue or morality is a necessary spring of popular government. The rule indeed extends with more or less force to every species of free Government. Who that is sincere friend to it, can look with indifference upon attempts to shake the foundation of the fabric."

George Washington, "Farewell Address," September 19, 1796, in George Washington: A Collection,
Compiled and Edited by W. B. Allen, (Indianapolis, IN: Liberty Classics, 1988), pp. 521-22.

Key Verses

Genesis 9:6
Deuteronomy 8:11-19
2 Chronicles 7:13-14
Judges 2:10-12; 17:6
Job 12:23
Psalms 2; 9:17; 33:12
Proverbs 8:15; 14:34; 29:2
Isaiah 9:6,7
Daniel 2:21; 4:31-32
Romans 13:1-7; 16:25-27
1 Peter 2:13-17

SUMMIT MINISTRIES

FACT SHEET

Summit Ministries
does not necessarily endorse all the views and
ideas represented by these sources.

PO BOX 207
MANITOU SPRINGS, CO 80829
(719) 685-9103

Need help teaching students to understand the times?
Help is at hand at the

summit student leadership conferences

Send your students to a summer conference that will change their life!   A SUMMIT experience will be unforgettable. They'll make great friends, ask all the questions they've been dying to ask, and learn how to be successful in life.   This will be the most intense, enjoyable and challenging two weeks your students have ever experienced.

what they will learn

THE SUMMIT is far more than a "summer camp" that provides only short-term motivation. At THE SUMMIT students will discover that a worldview based on God's Word is superior to other worldviews.   They will learn how to defend the Christian faith and live life with meaning and purpose from outstanding professors and well-known speakers from around the country.   Topics include

* Christian apologetics
* Courtship and marriage
* The Christian vs. Humanistic, New Age and Marxist worldviews
* Creation vs. Evolution
* America's Christian Heritage
* Free Market vs. Socialism
* A Biblical response to abortion and homosexuality
* Leadership and communication skills

In addition, a SUMMIT experience includes developing close friendships during "small group" time, participating in sports activities, going whitewater rafting and hiking, plus delicious meals.

> "I consider Summit Ministries to be one of the very best resources available, and I don't say that lightly!"
> Dr. James Dobson, Focus on the Family

two locations!

THE SUMMIT is currently being held in two locations.   The original SUMMIT at the foot of Pikes Peak in Colorado and SUMMIT EAST held on the campus of Bryan College in Dayton, Tennessee.   Both locations offer the option of earning two or three semester hours of college credit and the same quality teaching.   Recreation and optional activities vary at each location. Other locations are being added.

call today!

Call today for a brochure at the location of your choice.
Sessions fill quickly, so call SUMMIT MINISTRIES at 1-719-685-9103 (Monday -Friday, 9:00 a.m.-5:00 p.m. MST), or THE SUMMIT AT BRYAN COLLEGE at 1-423-775-7599 (Monday - Friday, 8:30 a.m.-5:00 p.m. EST).

> "Summit Ministries is wonderful.   It conveys to students how to think well as Christians.   It gives them a model of how to think critically and clearly about their faith.   Summit teaches them how to apply the Scriptures to their lives and be prepared for the issues they are going to face at the university."
> Dr. Francis Beckwith, Trinity International University

Resources for your youth from
Josh McDowell

1 Video Series for Youth

Setting You Free to Make Right Choices
Five-part Video Series featuring Josh McDowell

Through captivating video illustrations, dynamic teaching sessions, and creative group interaction, this series presents students with convincing evidence that right moral choices must be based on a standard outside of themselves. This powerful course equips your students with the understanding of what is right from what is wrong.

This series includes five video sessions, Leader's Guide with reproducible handout including samplers from the five "Right From Wrong" Workbooks, and the *Truth Slayers* book.

Setting You Free to Make Right Choices, Youth Video Series ISBN 0-8499-8585-4

2 Workbook for Junior High and High School Students

Setting You Free to Make Right Choices
by Josh McDowell with Leader's Guide

With a Bible-based emphasis, this Workbook creatively and systematically teaches your students how to determine right from wrong in their everyday lives – specifically applying the decision-making process to moral question about lying, cheating, getting even, and premarital sex.

Through eight youth group meetings followed each week with five daily exercises of 20-25 minutes per day, your teenagers will be challenged to develop a life-long habit of making right moral choices.

Setting You Free to Make Right Choices, Member's Workbook
ISBN 0-8054-9828-1

Setting You Free to Make Right Choices, Leader's Guide
ISBN 0-8054-9829-X

Contact your Christian supplier to obtain these "Right From Wrong" resources and begin to make it right in your home, your church, and your community.

notes & ideas